monday morning ®

KinderCenters
for Math Readiness

by Claudia Denny Vurnakes
illustrated by Marilynn G. Barr

Publisher: Roberta Suid
Copy Editor: Carol Whiteley
Production: Marilynn G. Barr

For a complete catalog, please write to the address below:
P.O. Box 1680, Palo Alto, California 94302

ISBN 1-878279-80-7

Printed in the United States of America

987654321

CONTENTS

Introduction

Manipulative, experiential, self-directed—these are the characteristics we aim for in planning activities for our early learners. Now you can make this type of independent learning a part of your preschool and kindergarten curriculum with *KinderCenters for Math Readiness*.

This book provides all of the patterns and activities you need for ten self-contained math learning centers with fairy tale themes. Each center focuses on a specific readiness skill, featuring five different activities that children can complete on their own. Student directions are given in picture form, so even the youngest child can "read" what to do. The activities are suitable for both independent and small-group work, giving you plenty of flexibility. And you can decide whether to have children complete one activity a day or work through an entire center at their own speed.

All ten centers in the book are based on favorite fairy tales. For added fun and enrichment you can connect the themes to other skill areas. For example, while your students work on numbers one to five with "Hansel and Gretel," they can be learning colors or discussing nutrition. Or you may choose to include a study of mothers and babies or discuss growth while working with the "Ugly Duckling" center. The fairy tale themes can also be extended to include dramatic play, art, music, movement, and playground activities.

It won't take a lot of time or artistic talent to make attractive learning centers—this book does the hard part for you. The patterns provided will make your centers visually exciting, and the student activities are ready to go. With the addition of a few easy-to-find materials, your learning centers will be complete, ready to provide hours of stimulating instruction. Be sure to read the construction and storage tips that follow for good ideas on making and managing your learning centers.

CONSTRUCTING THE LEARNING CENTERS

The learning centers described here are free-standing, folded panels. We recommend using three panels per center that measure approximately 19" x 24" each, but feel free to alter the dimensions to suit your classroom space and storage area. Use a stiff, strong material for your learning center panels—both corrugated cardboard and foam art board work well.

You may want to glue bright paper to the panels or spray-paint them to provide colorful, eye-catching backgrounds. Small art pieces are provided in each chapter that you can color and glue to the panels for additional appeal.

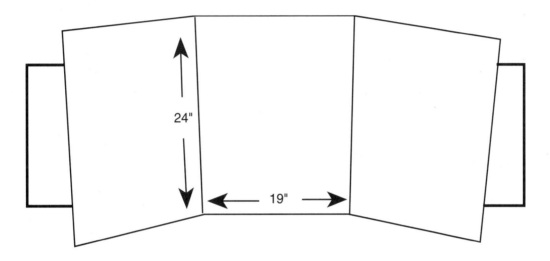

Hinge the panels together with durable tape at least two inches wide; duct tape is great for this. Position the panels so that you have a quarter- to a half-inch gap between them. Then tape the fronts and backs to make hinges that will allow you to fold the panels flat for storage. You may also want to tape the outside edges of the center to prevent frayed corners. The time you spend constructing a durable center will really pay off.

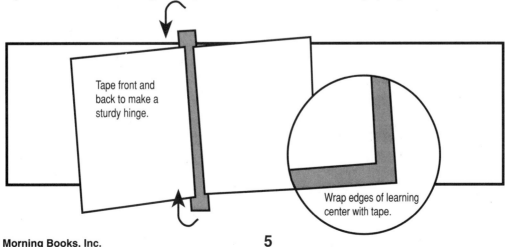

Tape front and back to make a sturdy hinge.

Wrap edges of learning center with tape.

ADDING SKILL PROGRAMMING

Duplicate the pages from this book for the learning center you want to make. Use markers, paint, or crayons to add color. Then cut out and glue the activities in position on your panels, using the illustration of the completed learning center at the front of the chapter as a guide.

For durable activity pieces, mount the pages on poster board and laminate before cutting them out. If you want to code the backs of pieces for self-checking, be sure to do that before you laminate.

STRONG CENTER MATERIALS

Most of the activities are manipulative, so you need to plan how you will store the materials. For pockets glued or stapled directly on the panels, use paper plates cut in half, small flat boxes, manila envelopes, or library card pockets. Some centers suggest other means of storing pieces, such as paper cups.

ADDITIONAL MATERIALS

All the materials necessary, in addition to those duplicated from the book, are easy to obtain, such as paper clips and pinch clothespins. A specific list of suggested materials is provided on the first page of each learning center chapter, but it is simple to adapt the activities to those supplies you have on hand. Several of the centers, for example, call for wipe-off pockets constructed from acetate transparencies. You could substitute any suitable clear film, or simply laminate the activity sheets so students can fill in their answers with a wipe-off crayon.

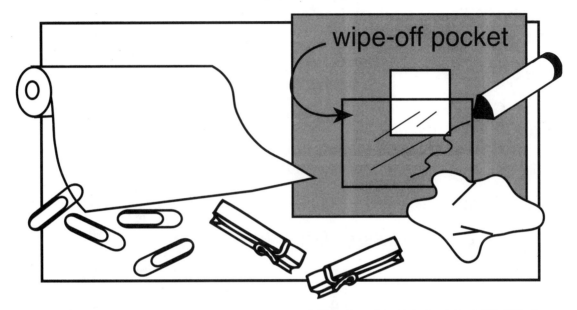

ADAPTING THE CENTERS TO OTHER SKILLS OR LEVELS

Many of the activities featured in this book can be adapted to other levels of difficulty, or used for different skills entirely. Just substitute your own student instruction boxes for the ones given with each activity and reprogram activity sheets for the desired skill. You can extend the life of a learning center by clipping new instructions over old ones.

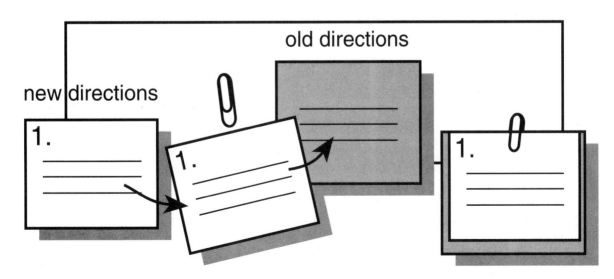

Resources

Adventures of Pinocchio by Carlo Collodi, translated by Marianna Mayer (Macmillan, 1981).

Aladdin, illustrated by Andrew Lang (Puffin Books, 1983).

Aladdin and His Wonderful Lamp by Leonard Lubin (Delacorte, 1982).

Aladdin and the Enchanted Lamp, illustrated by Marianna Mayer (Macmillan, 1985).

Anno's Aesop: A Book of Fables by Aesop and Mr. Fox, retold and illustrated by Mitsumasa Anno (Orchard Books Watts, 1989).

Cinderella by Charles Perrault, illustrated by Marcia Brown (Scribner's, 1954).

City Mouse, Country Mouse and Two More Tales from Aesop by John Wallner (Scholastic, 1987).

Fairy Tales, illustrated by Gyo Fujikawa (Putnam's, 1970).

Goldilocks and the Three Bears, illustrated by Jan Brett (Putnam's, 1987).

Hansel and Gretel by Rika Lesser (Dodd, 1984)

Little Red Riding Hood by Armand Eisen (Knopf, 1988).

Little Red Riding Hood by the Brothers Grimm, illustrated by Trina Schart Hyman (Holiday, 1983).

Pinocchio by Chris McEwan (Doubleday, 1990).

The Random House Book of Fairy Tales, adapted by Amy Ehrlich (Random, 1984).

The Tasha Tudor Book of Fairy Tales by Tasha Tudor (Putnam's, 1961).

The Three Bears and Fifteen Other Stories by Anne Rockwell (Crowell, 1975).

The Three Billy Goats Gruff, illustrated by Paul Galdone (Clarion, 1973).

The Tortoise and the Hare: An Aesop Fable, illustrated by Janet Stevens (Holiday, 1984).

The Town Mouse and the Country Mouse by Lorinda Bryan Cauley (Putnam's, 1986).

The Ugly Duckling by Hans Christian Anderson, illustrated by Robert Van Nutt (Knopf, 1986).

Hansel and Gretel

Numerals 1-5

Materials:

construction paper
transparency acetate
wipe-off crayons
2-inch brad
dish for counters
crayons
paste

masking tape
pinch clothespins
cleaning cloth
poster board
storage pockets
scissors

Hansel and Gretel

Hansel and Gretel

Hansel and Gretel

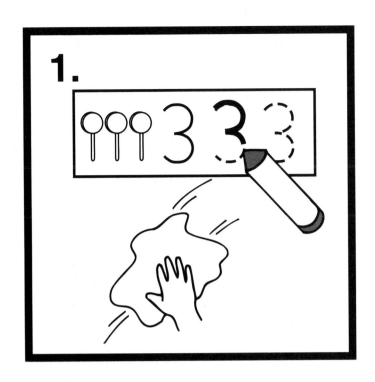

Hansel and Gretel

Writing Numerals

Directions:

Make a wipe-off pocket to hold numeral sheets. Cut one piece of transparency acetate and one piece of construction paper slightly larger than numeral sheet. Tape edges on three sides. Slide numeral sheet into pocket. Clip to center with clothespins. Provide wipe-off crayon and cleaning cloth. Update center by changing numeral sheets.

Students use crayons to trace numerals.

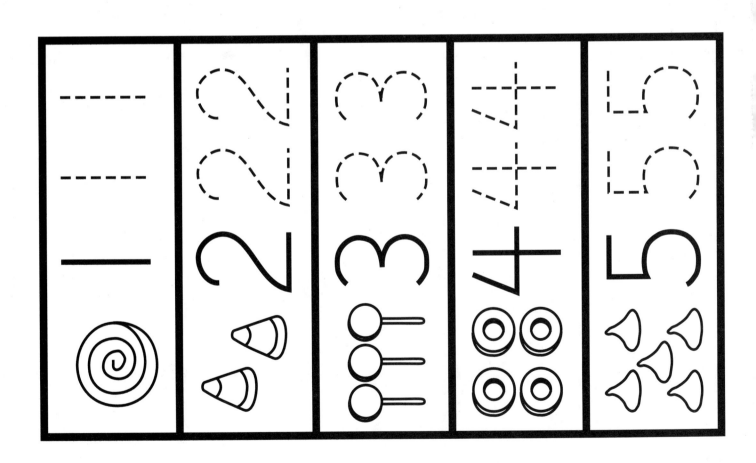

Hansel and Gretel

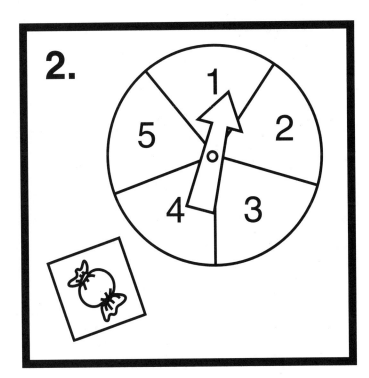

Hansel and Gretel
Counting

Directions:
Duplicate candy counters on page 16. Color and cut apart. Store in dish in front of center. Color and mount numeral wheel on center. Mount arrow on poster board and attach to wheel with 2-inch brad.

Students spin a numeral and count out the correct number of candy counters.

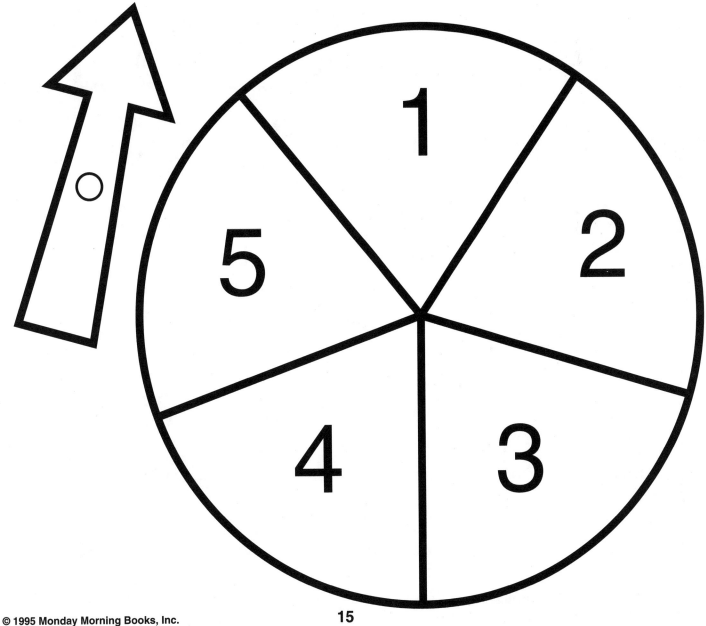

Hansel and Gretel

Counting to Match a Set

3.

Directions:

Duplicate dot patterns below. Cut apart and store in pocket on center.

Students use dot patterns and counters from dish (see activity #2) to make matching sets.

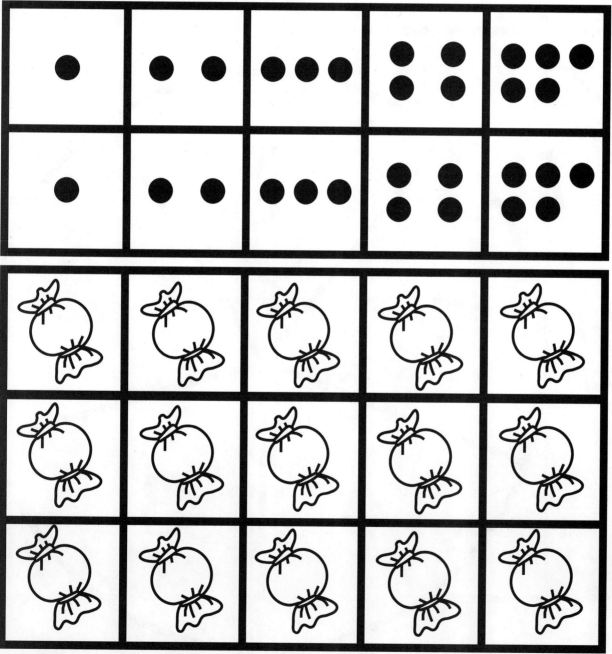

Hansel and Gretel
Writing Numerals

Directions:
Make wipe-off pocket to hold counting sheets. Cut one piece of transparency acetate and one piece of construction paper slightly larger than counting sheet. Tape edges on three sides. Slide sheet into pocket and clip to center with clothespins. Provide wipe-off crayon and cleaning cloth. Update center by changing counting sheets.

Students count objects and write numerals.

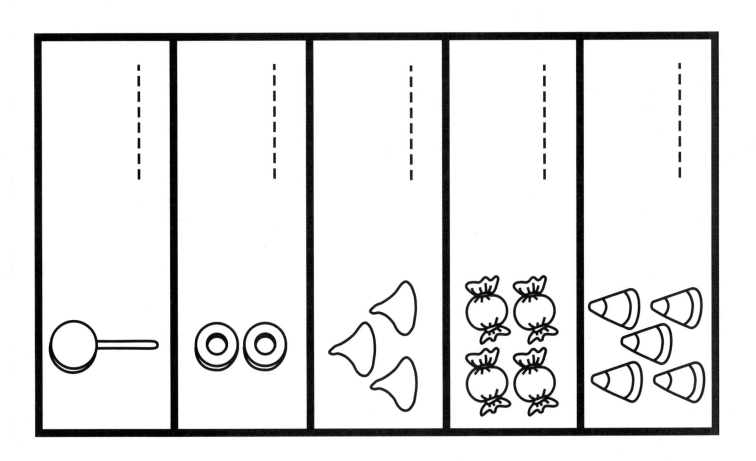

Hansel and Gretel

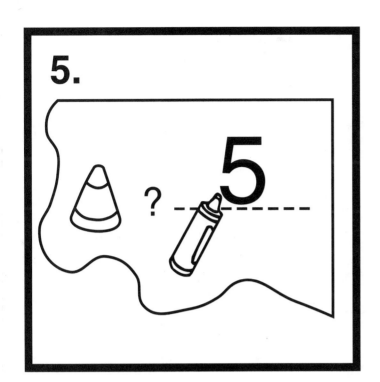

Hansel and Gretel
Counting Items in Larger Set

Directions:

Duplicate question sheet below. Store copies in pocket on center. Color and mount Gingerbread House (page 20) on center.

Students count items in scene to complete question sheet.

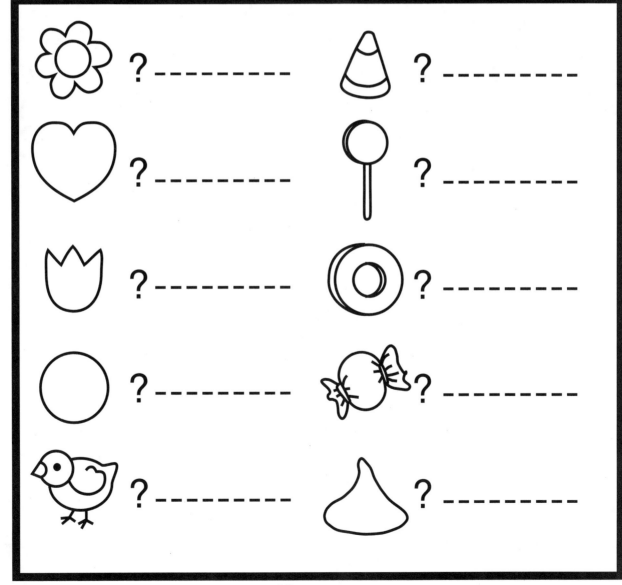

Gingerbread House

20

Cinderella

Numerals 6-10

Materials:

pinch clothespins	wipe-off crayons
construction paper	transparency acetate
2-inch brad	crayons
poster board	masking tape
cleaning cloth	storage pockets
scissors	glue, paste

21

Cinderella

Cinderella

Cinderella

24

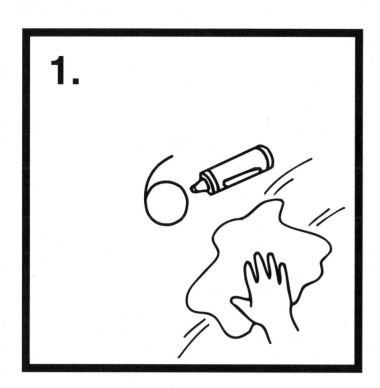

1.

Cinderella
Writing Numerals

Directions:
Make wipe-off pocket to hold activity sheet. Cut one piece of transparency acetate and one piece of construction paper slightly larger than activity sheet. Tape edges on three sides with masking tape. Slide activity sheet into pocket. Clip to center with clothespins. Provide wipe-off crayon and cleaning cloth. Update center by placing new activity sheet in wipe-off pocket.

Students trace numerals.

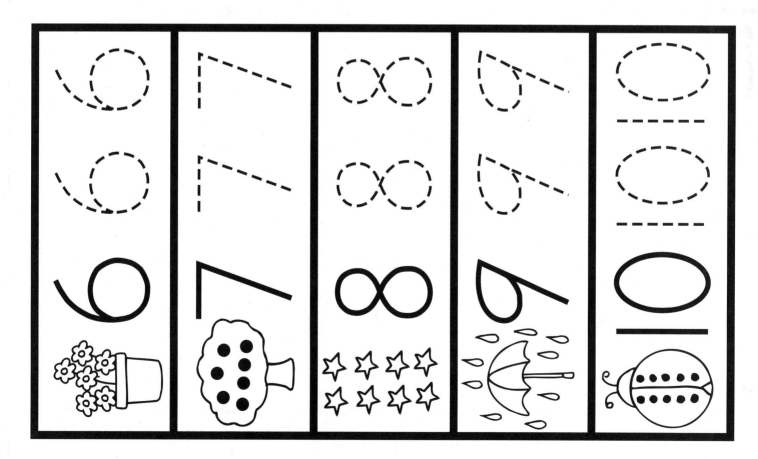

Cinderella

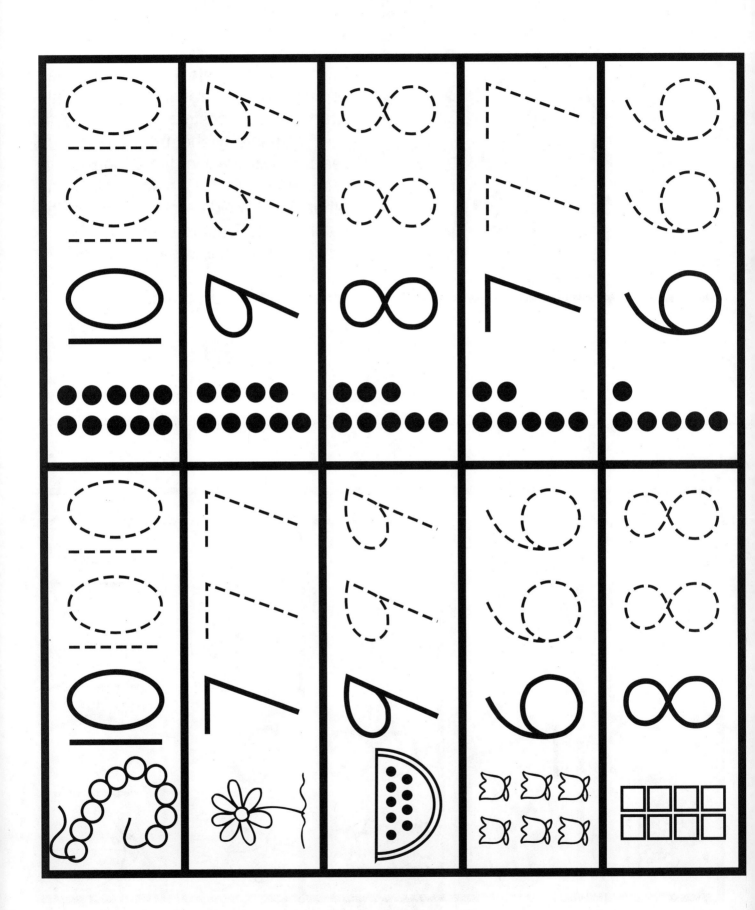

Cinderella
Counting

Directions:
Use pumpkin counters on page 28. Mount on poster board and cut apart. Store in pocket on center. Paste numeral wheel to center. Mount arrow on poster board and attach to wheel with 2-inch brad.

Students spin and count out the correct number of pumpkins.

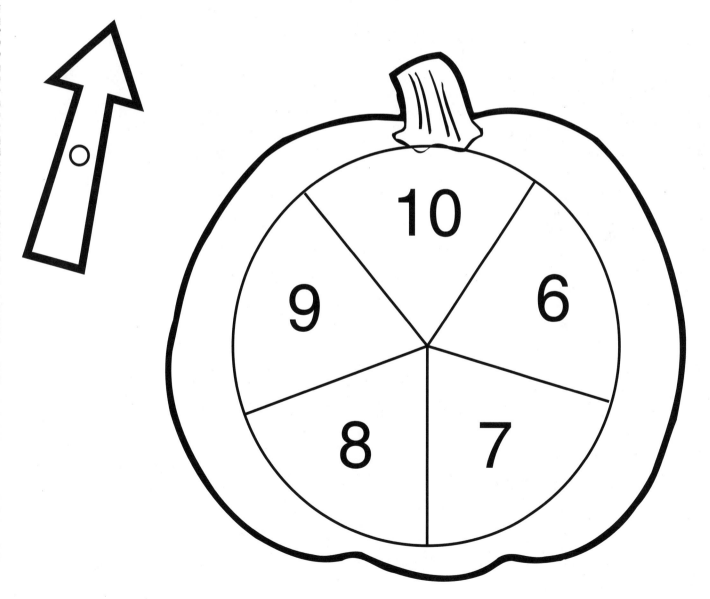

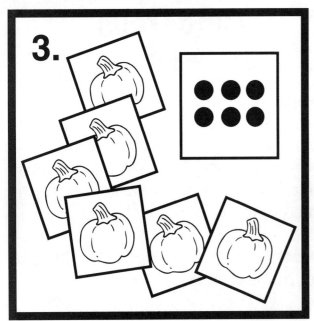

Cinderella
Counting to Match a Set

Directions:
Mount dots and pumpkins on poster board. Cut apart and store in separate pockets on center.

Students choose a dot card, then count out the correct number of pumpkins.

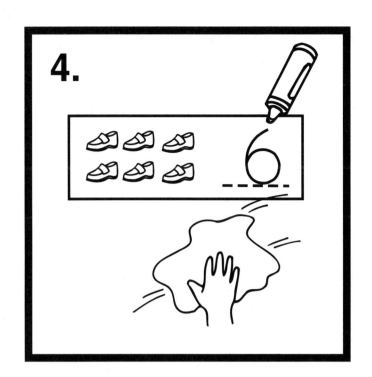

Cinderella
Counting and Writing Numerals

Directions:
Make wipe-off pocket to hold activity sheet. Cut one piece of transparency acetate and one piece of construction paper slightly larger than activity sheet. Tape edges on three sides with masking tape. Slide activity sheet into pocket. Clip to center with clothespins. Provide wipe-off crayon and cleaning cloth. Update center by placing new activity sheet in wipe-off pocket.

Students count objects and write correct numeral.

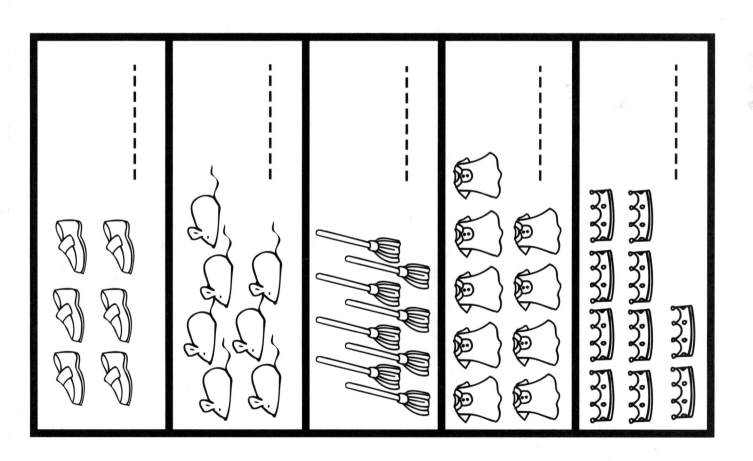

Cinderella

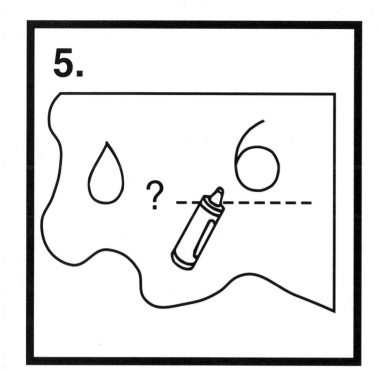

5.

Cinderella
Counting Numerals from Larger Set

Directions:
Duplicate tally sheets and store in pocket on center. Color pumpkin patch (page 32). Mount on center. Provide crayons.

Students count shapes in picture to complete tally sheets.

The Tortoise and the Hare

Numerals 1-10

Materials:

storage pockets

paste

paper cup

scissors

2-inch brad

crayons

poster board

The Tortoise and the Hare

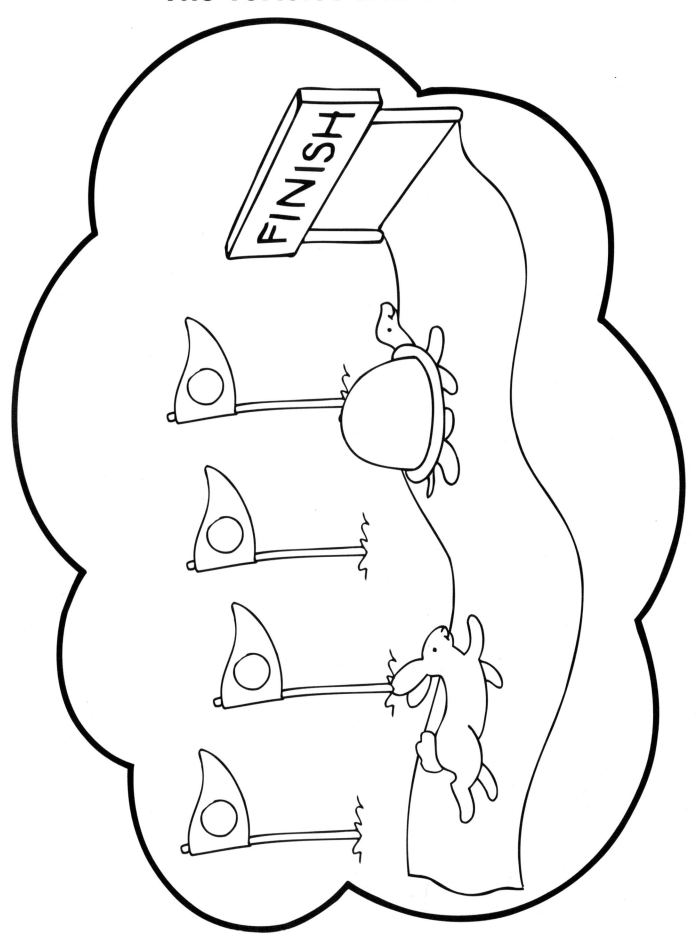

35

The Tortoise and the Hare

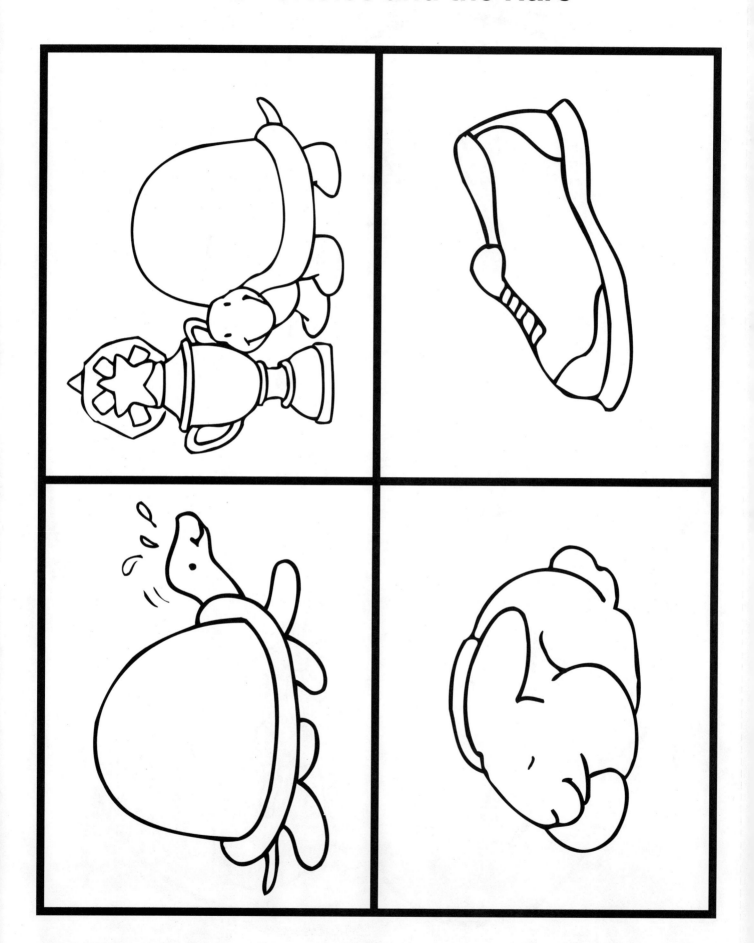

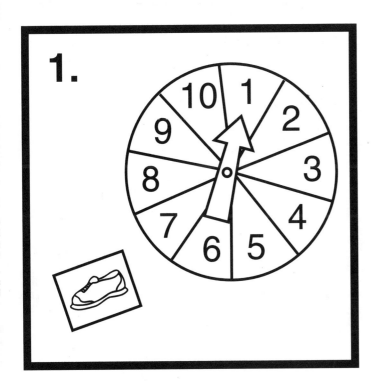

The Tortoise and the Hare

Spinning Numerals and Counting

Directions:
Paste numeral wheel to center. Mount arrow on poster board and attach to wheel with 2-inch brad. Duplicate sneaker counters on page 38 and cut apart. Store in pocket on center.

Students spin and count out the correct number of sneakers.

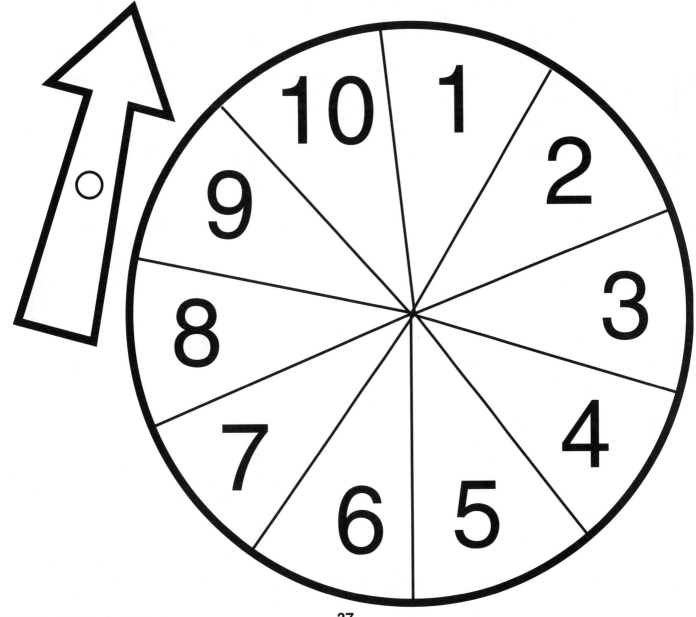

The Tortoise and the Hare

38

2.

The Tortoise and the Hare

Matching Numerals to Sets

Directions:
Mount numeral and set cards on poster board. Laminate, cut apart, and store in separate pockets on center. If self-checking is desired, color-code backs of cards prior to laminating.

Students match numerals to sets.

1	2	3	4
5	6	7	8
9	10		

The Tortoise and the Hare

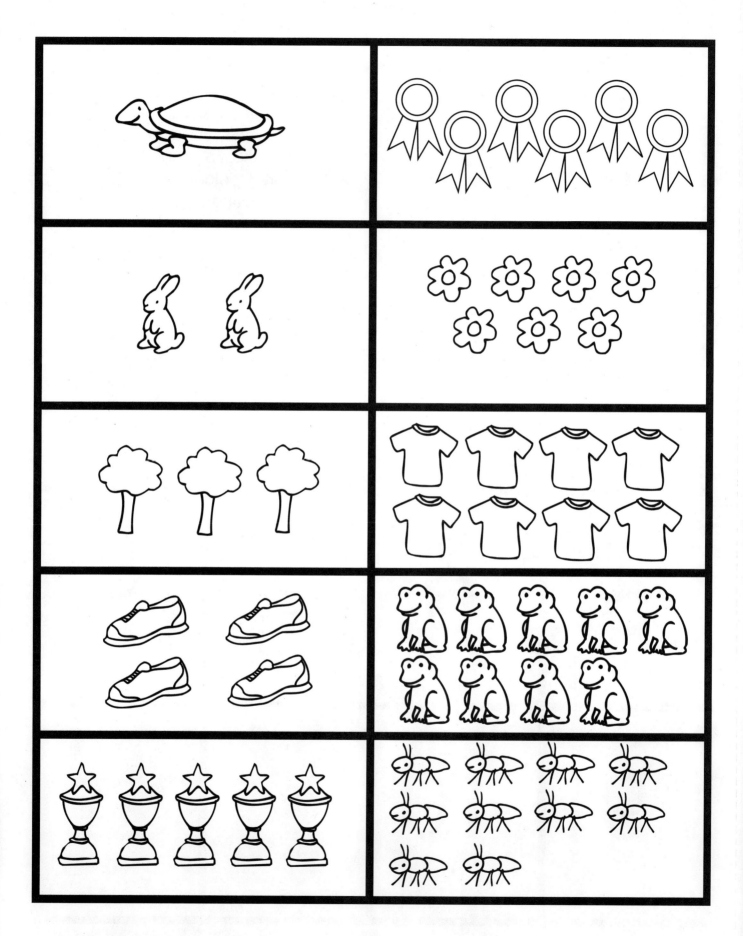

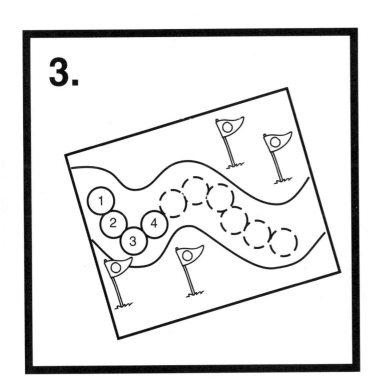

The Tortoise
and the Hare

Placing Numerals in Sequence

Directions:

Color and mount numeral circles and race track (page 42) on poster board and laminate. Cut out circles; store in paper cup placed in front of center. Place race track in large pocket on center.

Students place numerals in sequence on the track.

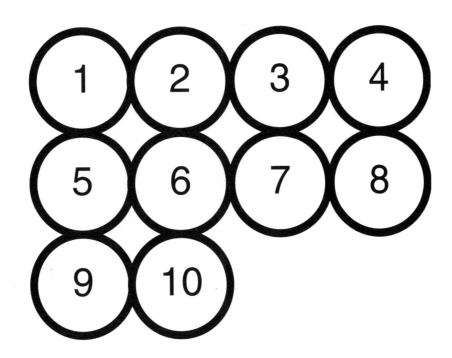

The Tortoise and the Hare

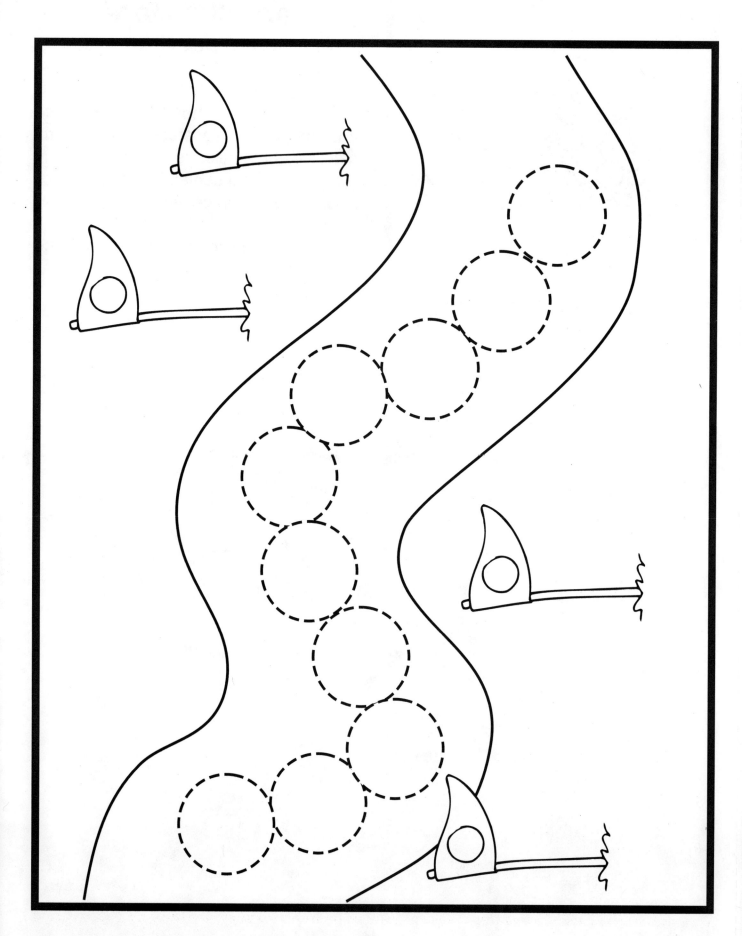

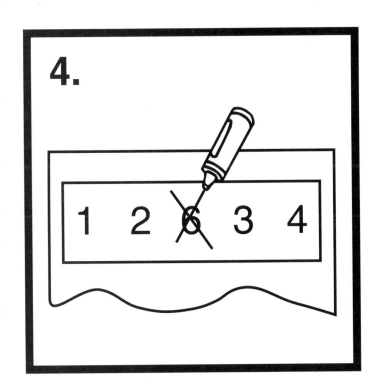

The Tortoise and the Hare

Crossing Out Numerals
That Are Out of Order

Directions:
Duplicate activity sheets and store in pocket on center. Provide crayons.

Students cross out the numbers that are out of order in each row.

The Tortoise and the Hare

2 3 7 4   7 6 8 9

6 7 3 8   8 9 10 7

2 4 5 6   5 4 6 7

1 2 5

10

3

8

4

9

6   6 8 7

5 6 7

44

5.

The Tortoise and the Hare

Connecting Dots in Correct Sequence

Directions:
Duplicate dot-to-dot drawings and store in pocket on center. Provide crayons for students to use.

Students connect dots in sequence.

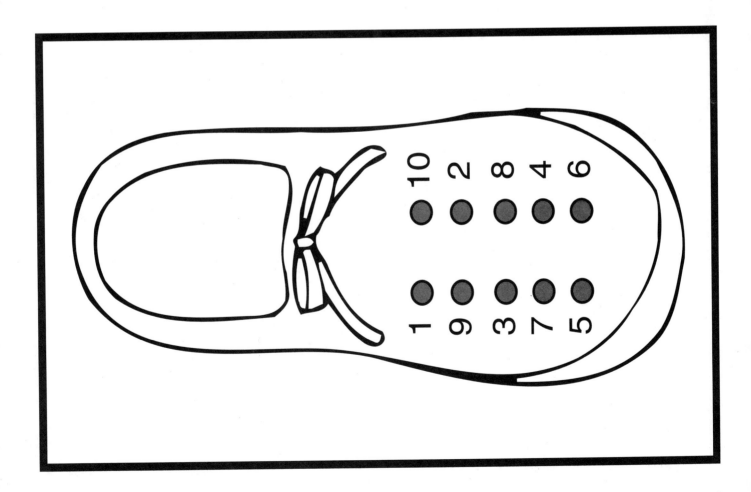

The Tortoise and the Hare

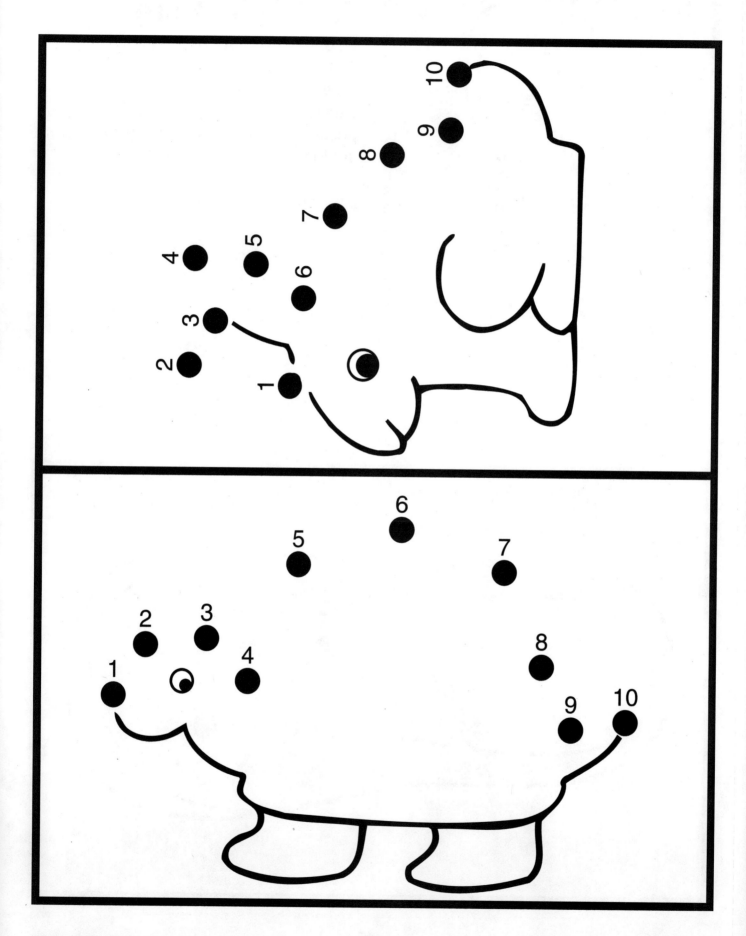

Little Red Riding Hood
Comparing Numerals 1-10

Materials:

storage pockets	cleaning cloth
stapler, staples	poster board
wipe-off crayons	crayons
scissors	paste

Little Red

Riding Hood

Little Red Riding Hood

Little Red Riding Hood

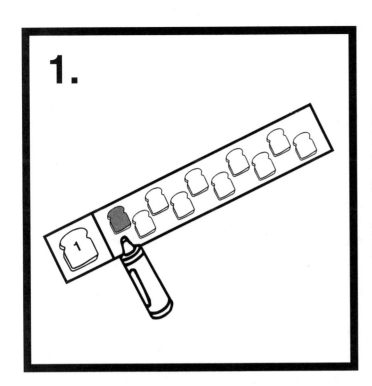

Little Red Riding Hood

Counting to Color

Directions:
Duplicate activity strips and cut apart. Store in pocket on center. Provide crayons for students to use.

Students color the correct number of items.

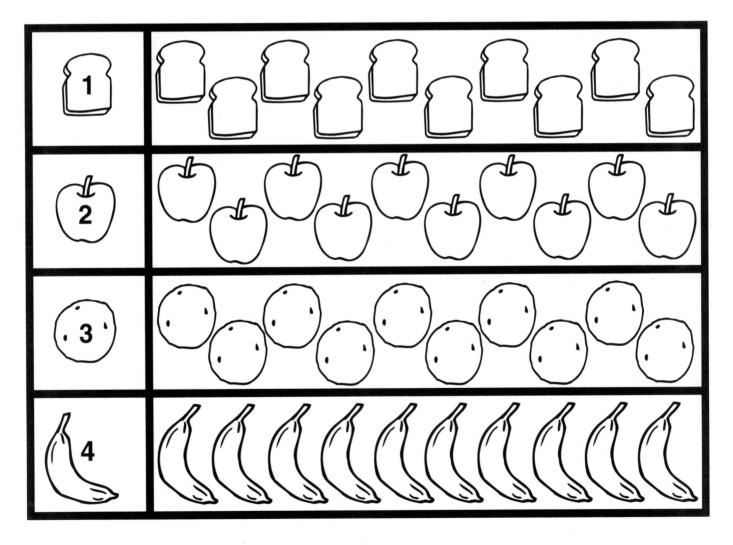

Little Red Riding Hood

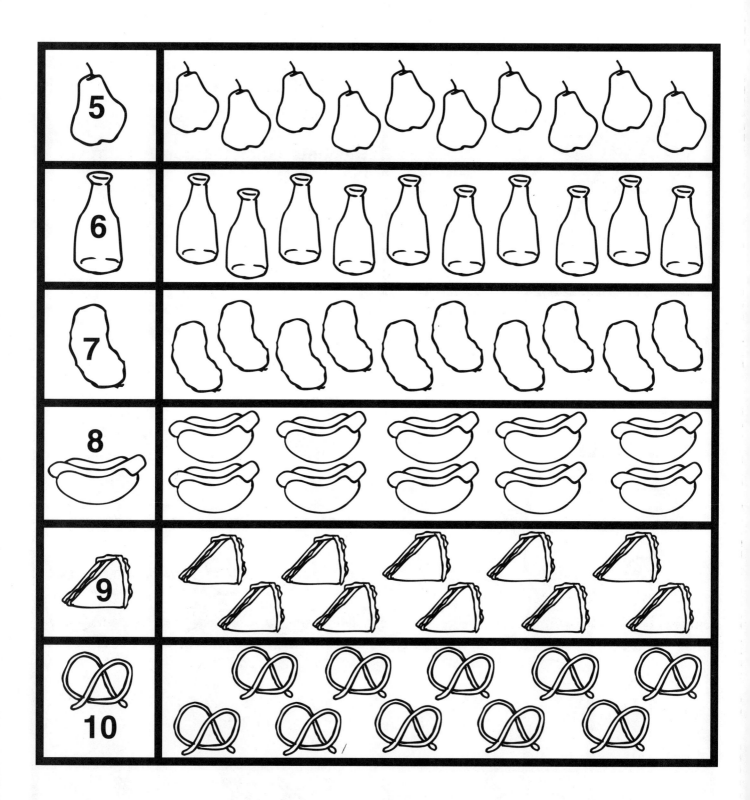

Little Red Riding Hood
Matching Sets

Directions:
Mount puzzle cards on poster board, laminate, and cut apart. Store in pocket on center.

Students match pictures to dots.

Little Red Riding Hood

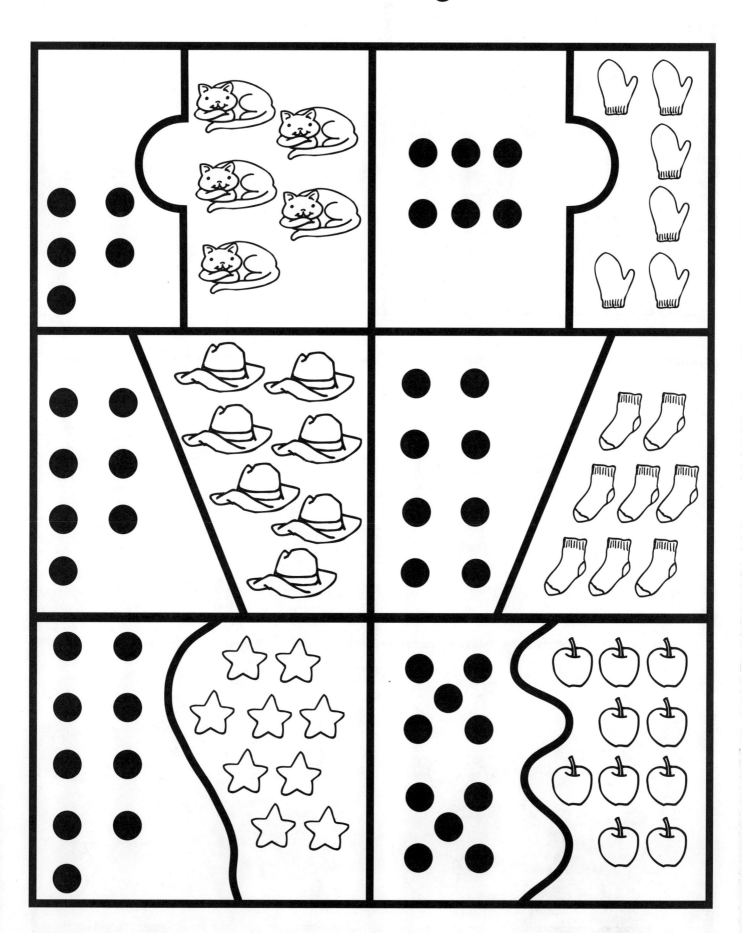

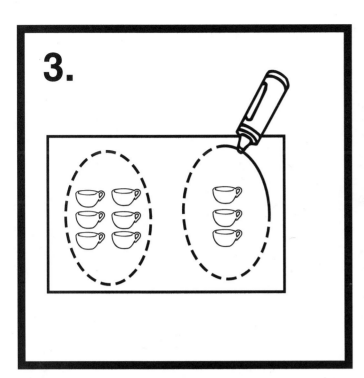

3.

Little Red Riding Hood
Choosing Smaller of Two Sets

Directions:
Duplicate activity pages, cut apart, and staple together to make small booklets. Store in pocket on center. Provide crayons for students to use.

Students circle the smaller set on each page.

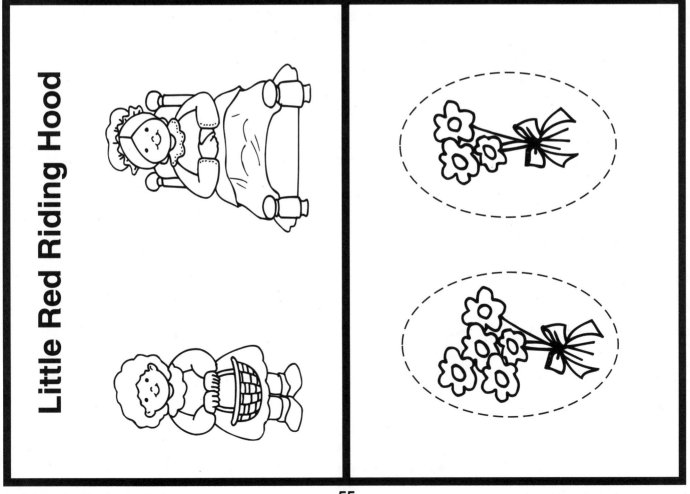

Little Red Riding Hood

Little Red Riding Hood

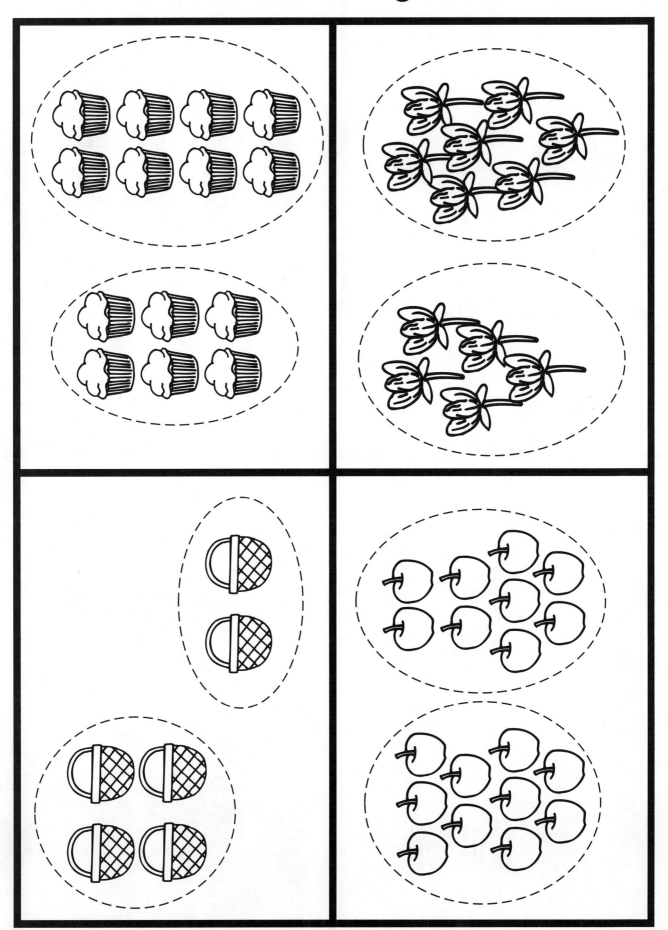

56

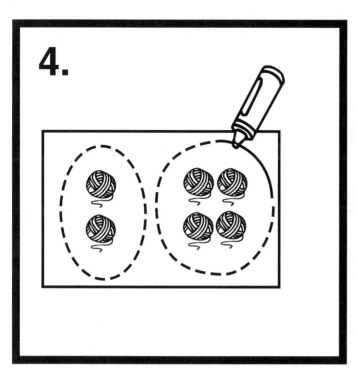

4.

Little Red Riding Hood
Choosing Larger of Two Sets

Directions:
Duplicate activity pages, cut apart, and staple together to make small booklets. Store in pocket on center. Provide crayons for students to use.

Students circle the larger.

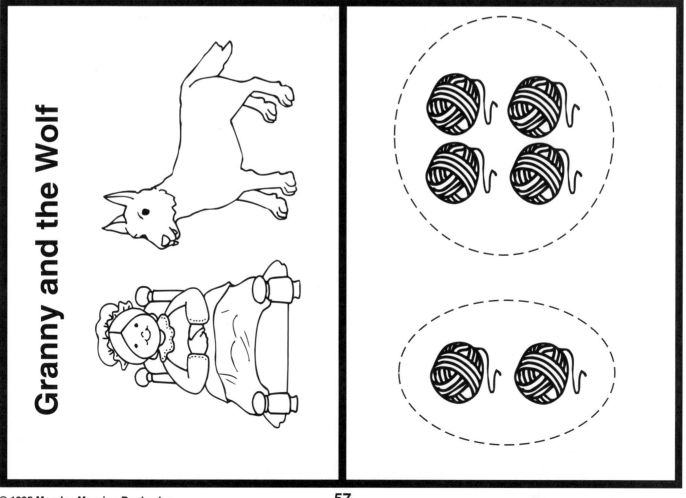

Granny and the Wolf

Little Red Riding Hood

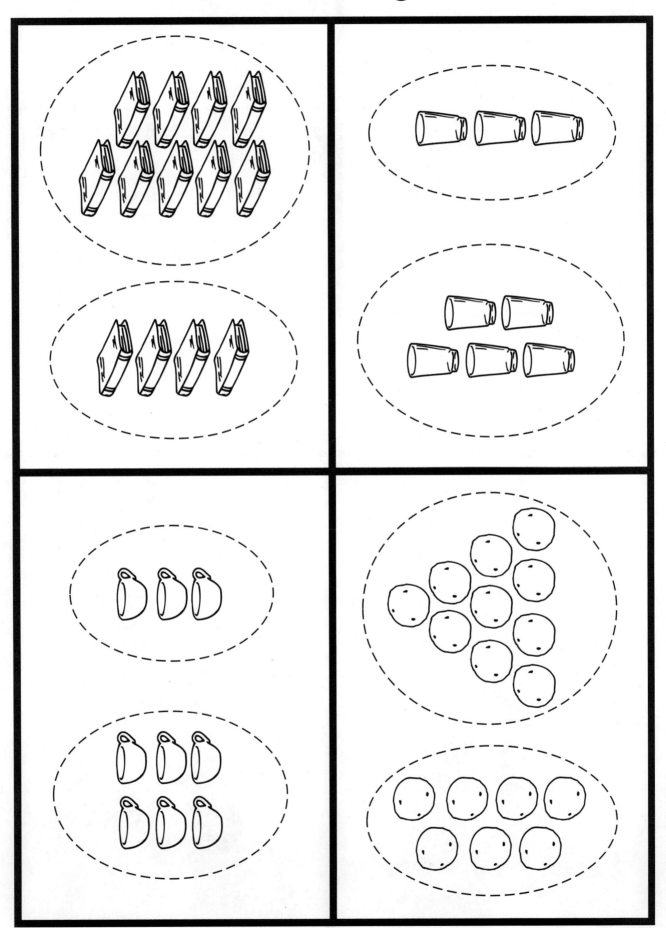

58

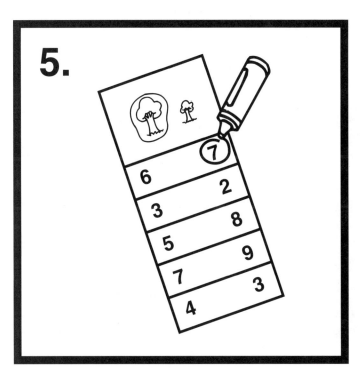

5.

Little Red Riding Hood
Choosing Larger or Smaller of Two Sets

Directions:
Duplicate activity strips, laminate, and cut apart. Store in pocket on center. Provide wipe-off crayons for students to use.

Students circle the larger or smaller numbers according to each strip.

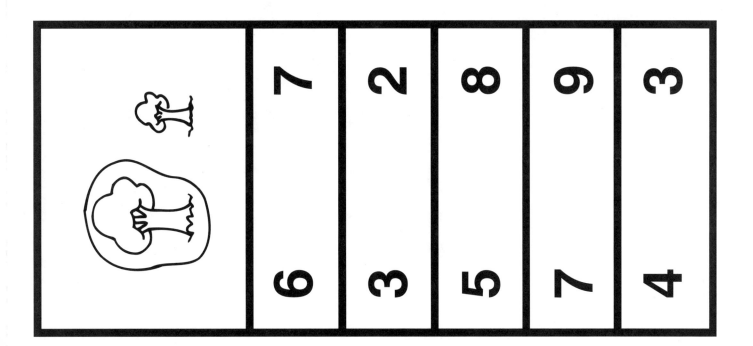

Little Red Riding Hood

2 5	7 6	2 1	8 10	7 9
4 3	9 7	4 6	10 9	5 8
2 1	3 5	5 6	10 7	4 8

Pinocchio
Numeral Words 1-10

Materials:

pinch clothespins	transparency acetate
wipe-off crayons	storage pockets
paper clip	poster board
construction paper	masking tape
cleaning cloth	hole punch
short pencil	scissors
paste	crayons

61

Pinocchio

Pinocchio

Pinocchio

64

Pinocchio

Writing Numeral Words

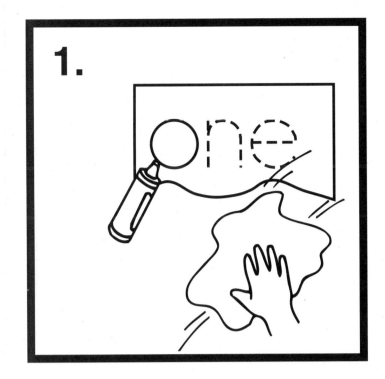

Directions:

Make wipe-off pocket to hold activity sheet. Cut one piece of transparency acetate and one piece of construction paper slightly larger than the activity sheet. Tape edges on three sides with masking tape. Slide activity sheet into pocket. Clip to center with clothespins. Provide wipe-off crayon and cleaning cloth. Update center by placing new activity sheet in wipe-off pocket.

Students trace or write numeral words.

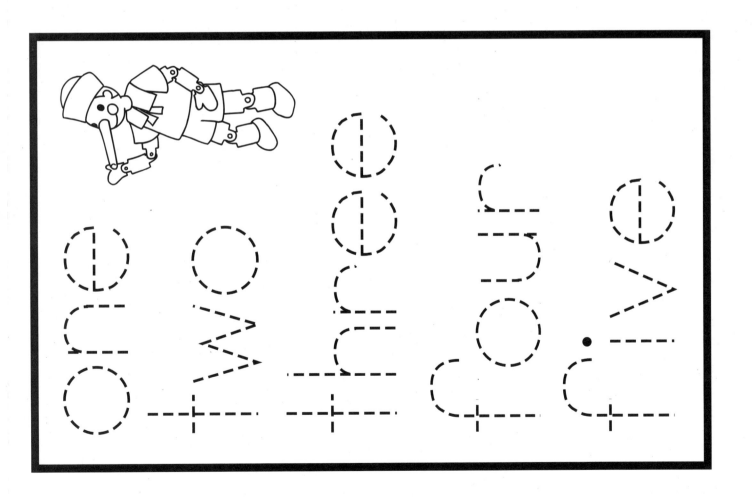

65

Pinocchio

_ne   fi_e   ni_e

tw_   si_   t_n

thr_e   _even

f_ur   eigh_

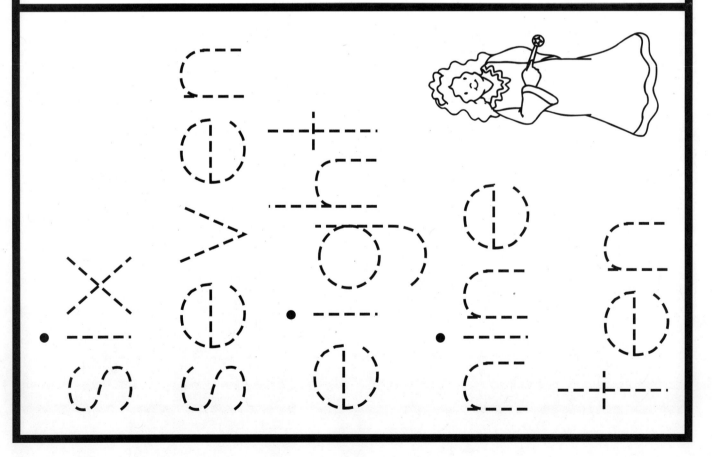

Pinocchio
Circling Correct Numeral Word

Directions:
Duplicate numeral sheets. Cut apart and store in pocket on center. Provide crayons for students to use.

Students circle correct answers.

three one	two six	four five	four ten	seven six

Pinocchio

nine / ten	two / three	one / ten	three / seven	five / two

five / eight	eight / nine	two / ten	three / six	four / eight

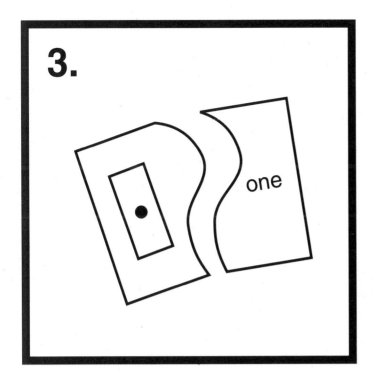

Pinocchio
Matching Numeral Words to Sets

Directions:
Mount puzzle cards on poster board. Cut apart and store in pocket on center.

Students match numeral words to sets.

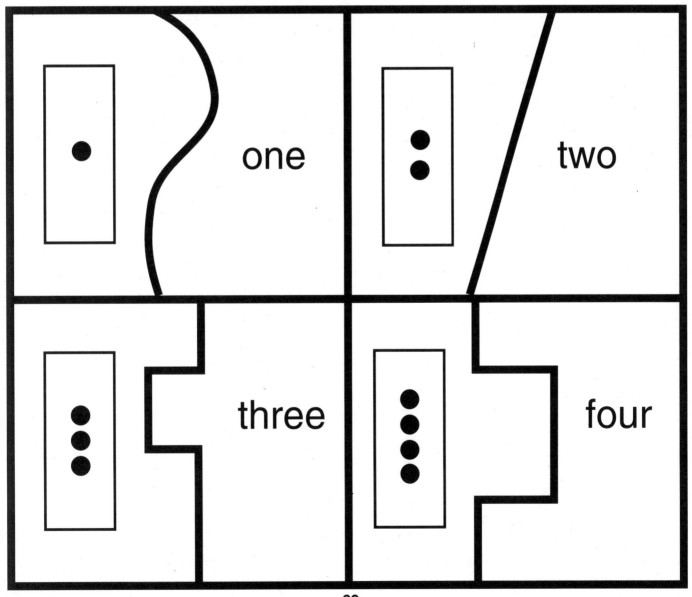

Pinocchio

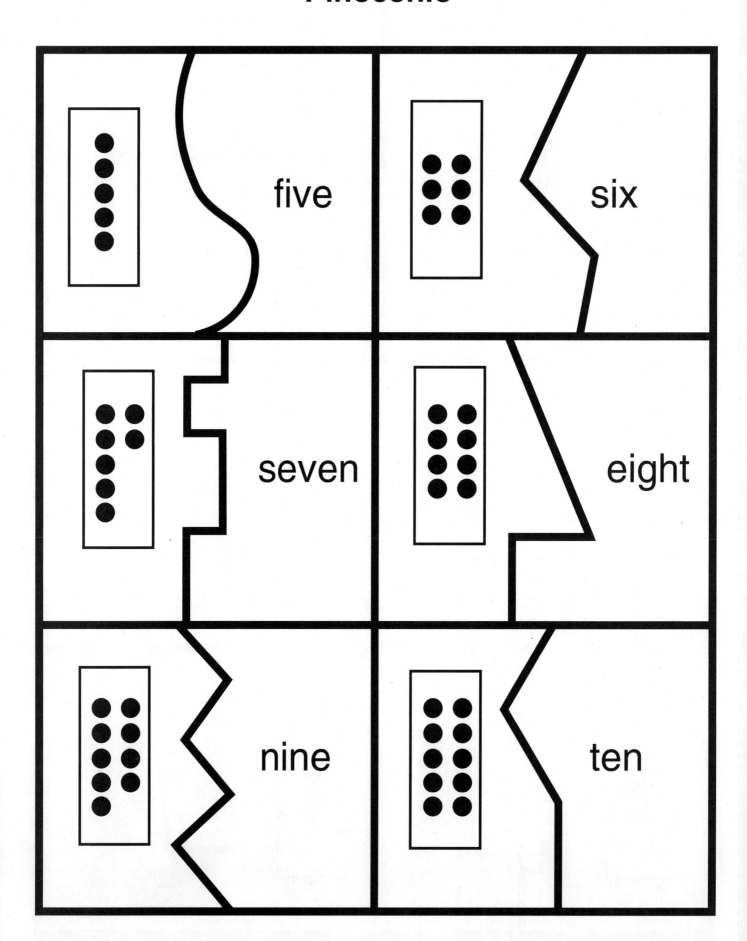

five

six

seven

eight

nine

ten

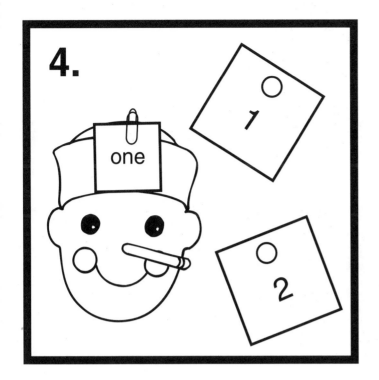

Pinocchio
Matching Words and Numerals

Directions:
Mount face on poster board and cut out. Slip paper clip on top of cap as shown: paste face to center. Poke pencil point through face and center at the X to form Pinocchio's nose. Mount numeral and word cards on poster board. Cut apart, punch holes in numeral cards, and store cards in separate pockets on center.

Students clip each word card on Pinocchio's cap and hang matching numeral card on nose.

Pinocchio

one	two	three	four
five	six	seven	eight
nine	ten	○ 1	○ 2
○ 3	○ 4	○ 5	○ 6
○ 7	○ 8	○ 9	○ 10

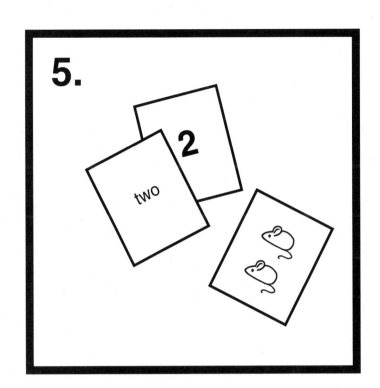

Pinocchio

Matching Words, Numerals, and Sets

Directions:
Make word and numeral cards to go with set cards. Mount all cards on poster board. Laminate, cut apart, and store in pocket on center.

Students match cards to make complete sets.

Pattern for
Word and
Numeral Cards

Pinocchio

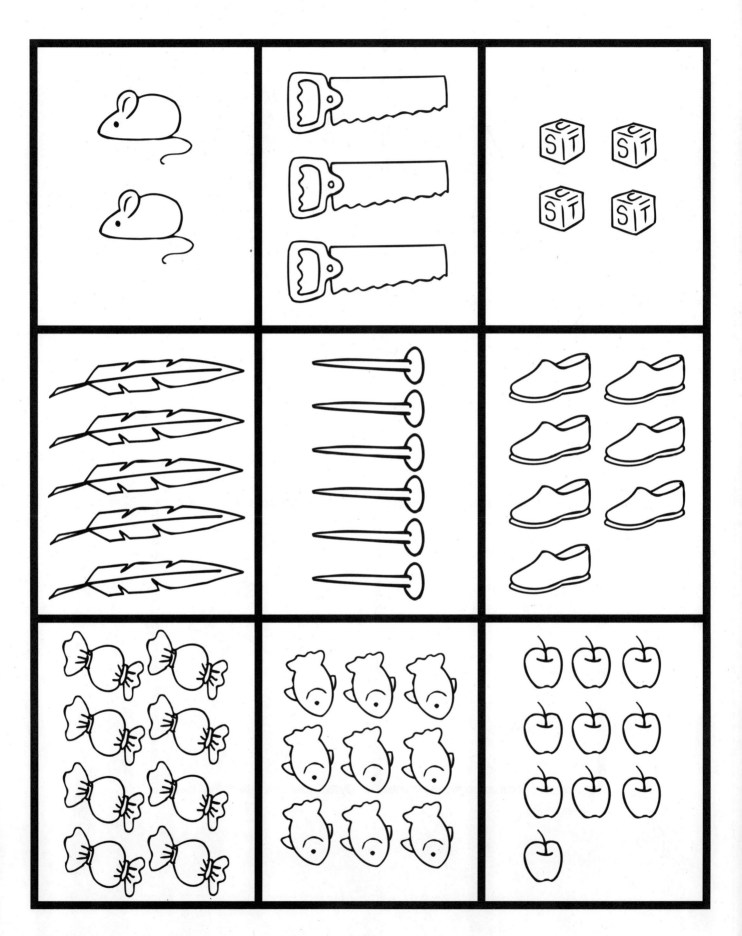

The Billy Goats Gruff

Shapes

The Billy Goats Gruff

Billy Goats Gruff

Materials:

zip-lock plastic bags　　storage pockets
magnetic tape　　　　　crayons
pinch clothespins　　　　paper clips
2-inch brad　　　　　　stapler, staples
poster board　　　　　　paste
scissors　　　　　　　　construction paper

The Billy Goats Gruff

The Billy Goats Gruff

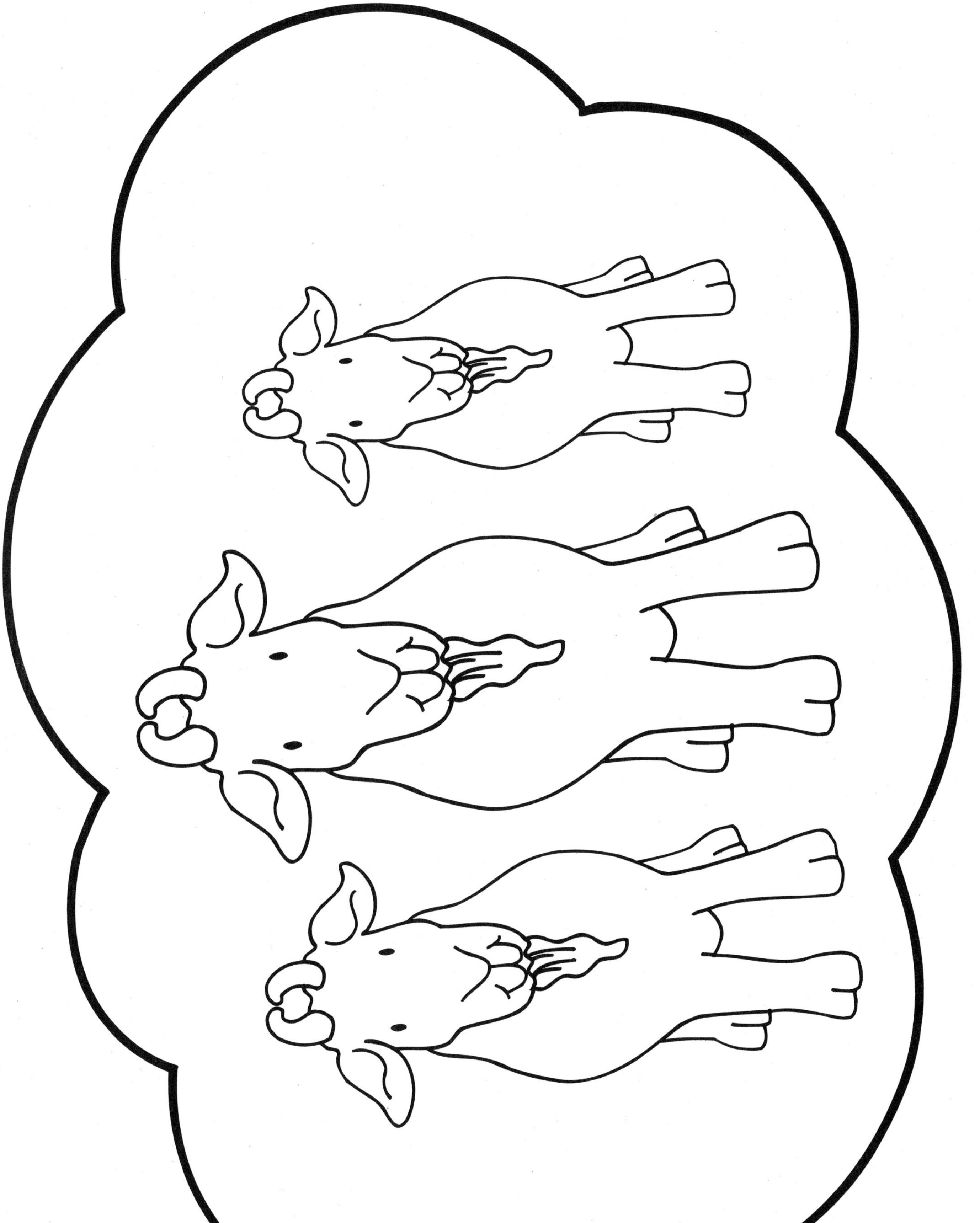

The Billy Goats Gruff

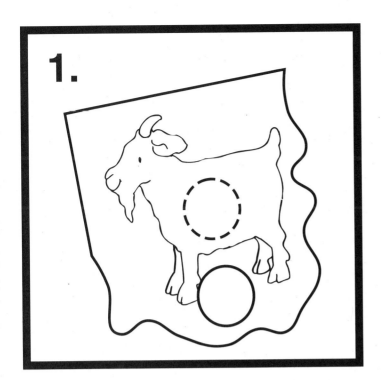

The Billy Goats Gruff
Matching Circles and Triangles

Directions:
Color puzzle sheet (page 80), circles, and triangles. Mount on poster board and laminate. Cut out circles and triangles. Place in zip-lock bag and clip to puzzle with clothespin. Store in pocket on center.

Students place cutouts on correct place on puzzle.

The Billy Goats Gruff

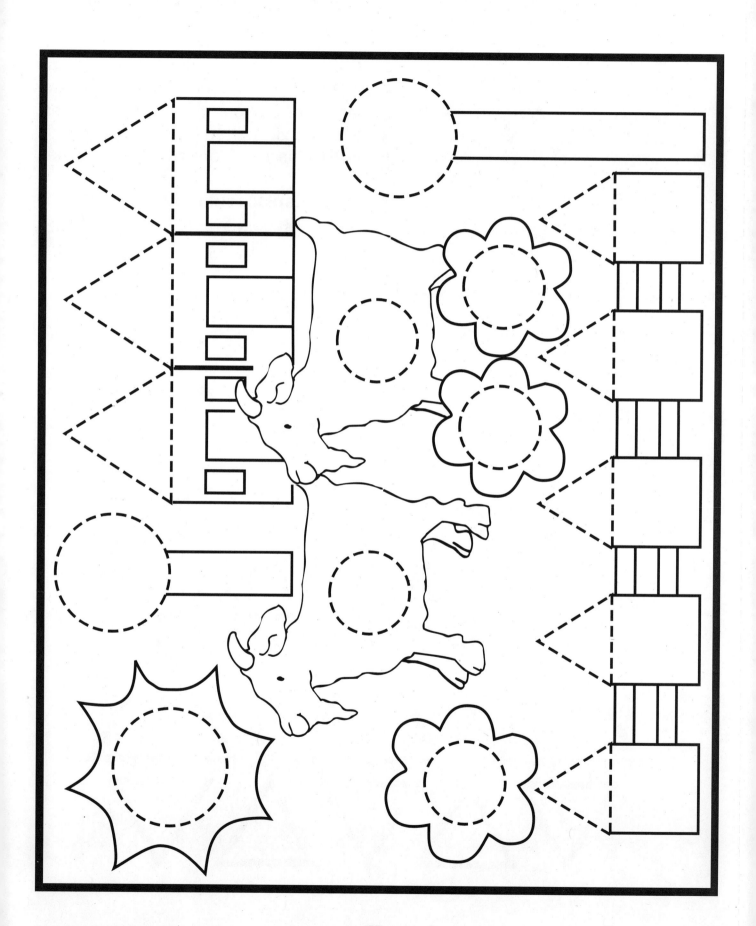

80

2.

The Billy Goats Gruff
Matching Squares and Rectangles

Directions:
Color puzzle sheet (page 82), squares, and rectangles. Mount on poster board and laminate. Cut out squares and rectangles. Place in zip-lock bag and clip to puzzle with clothespin. Store in pocket on center.

Students place cutouts on correct place on puzzle.

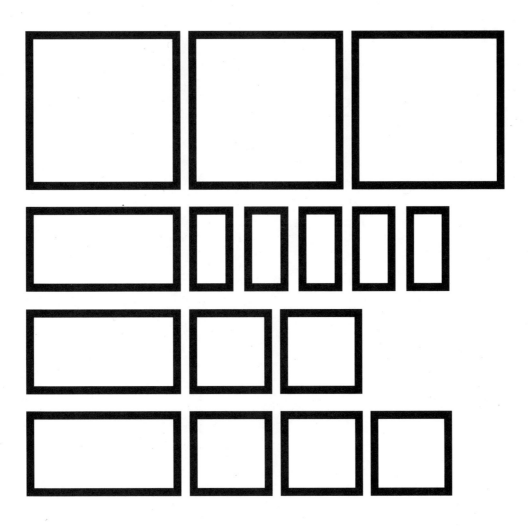

The Billy Goats Gruff

82

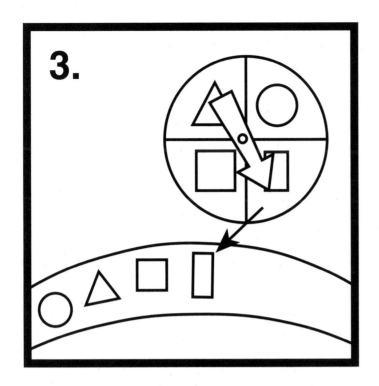

The Billy Goats Gruff
Choosing the Correct Shape

Directions:
Color shape wheel. Paste shape wheel to center. Mount arrow on poster board and attach to wheel with 2-inch brad. Cut bridge from construction paper and paste on center. Position squares of magnetic tape along bridge. Color shape page, mount on poster board, laminate, and cut apart. Slide paper clip on each cutout. Store cutouts in pocket on center.

Students spin, then place indicated shape on bridge.

The Billy Goats Gruff

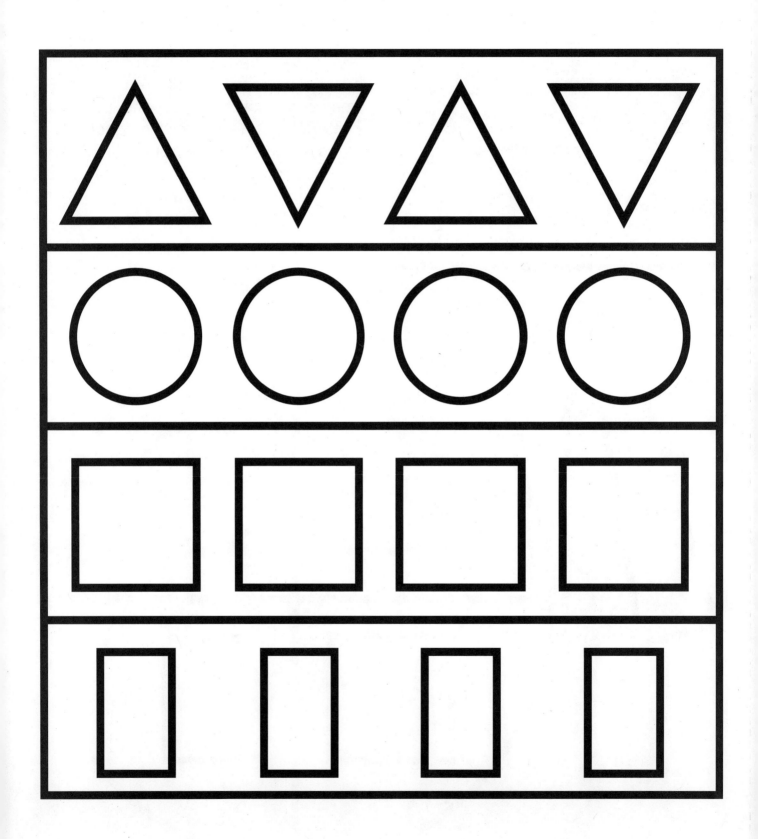

4.

The Billy Goats Gruff
Coloring Shapes

Directions:
Add indicated colors to direction card. Mount on center. Duplicate activity sheet (page 86)and store in pocket on center. Provide crayons for students to use.

Students color shapes to match card.

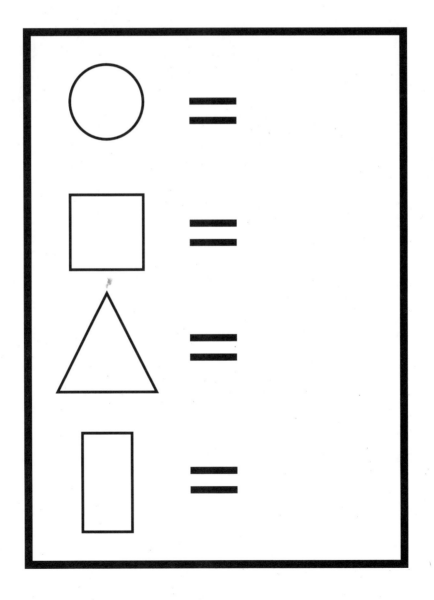

The Billy Goats Gruff

5.

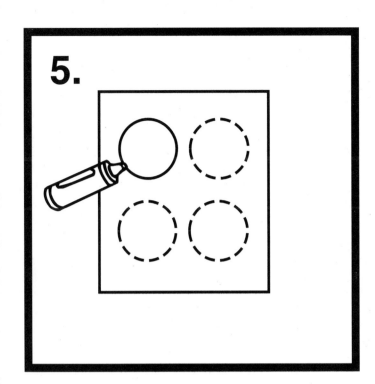

The Billy Goats Gruff
Drawing Shapes

Directions:
Duplicate activity sheets. Cut apart and staple to form booklets. Store in pocket on center. Provide crayons for students to use.

Students trace shapes.

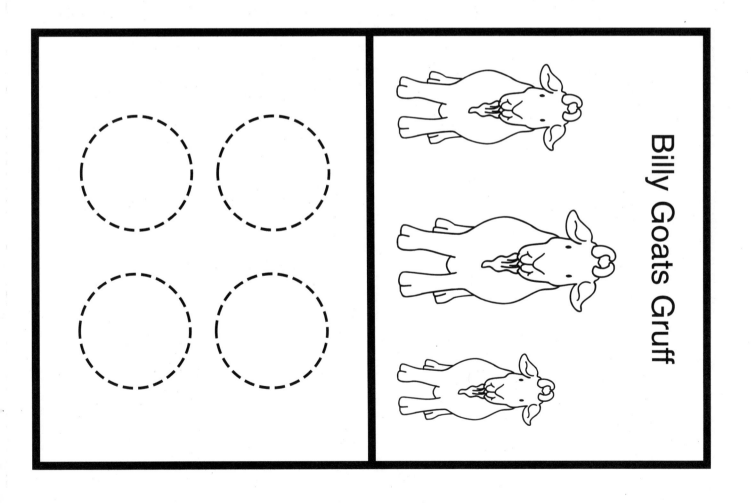

Billy Goats Gruff

The Billy Goats Gruff

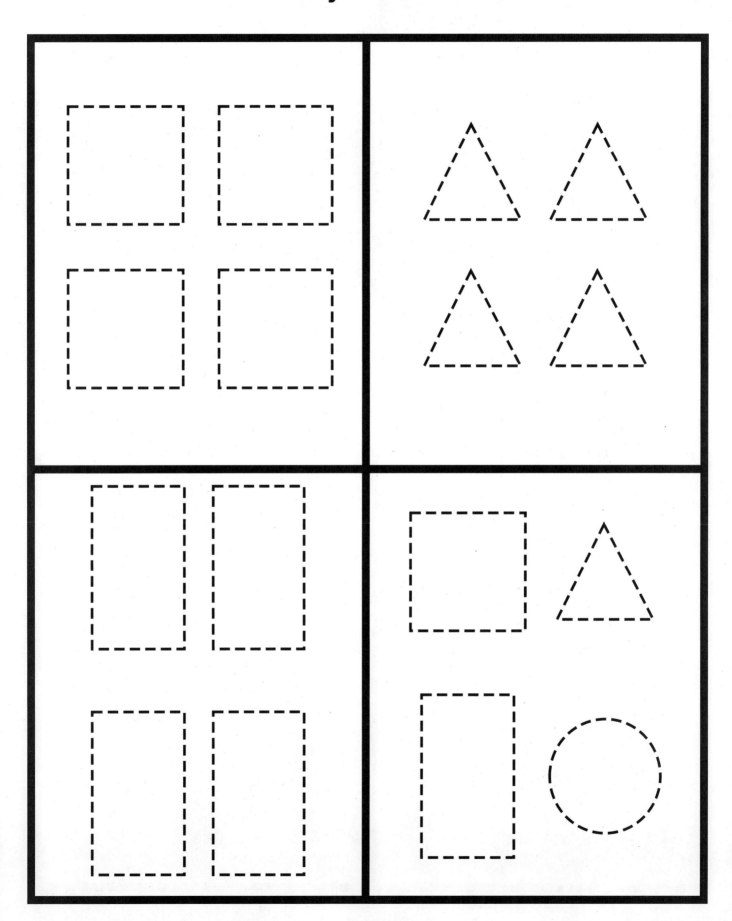

88

Aladdin

Days of the Week

Materials:

masking tape	transparency acetate
wipe-off crayon	scissors
crayons	zip-lock bags
construction paper	pinch clothespins
cleaning cloth	paste
storage pockets	poster board

Aladdin

Aladdin

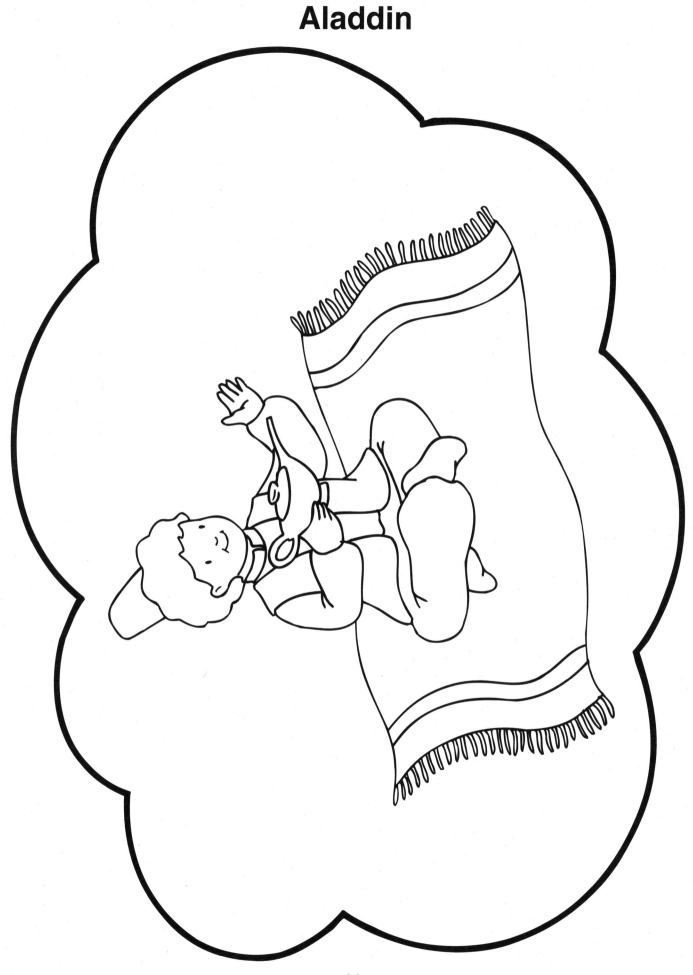

Aladdin

Aladdin
Writing Days of the Week

Directions:
Make wipe-off pocket to hold activity sheet. Cut one piece of transparency acetate and one piece of construction paper slightly larger than activity sheet. Tape edges on three sides with masking tape. Slide activity sheet into pocket. Clip to center with clothespins. Provide wipe-off crayon and cleaning cloth. Update center by placing new activity sheet in wipe-off pocket.

Students trace days of the week.

Aladdin

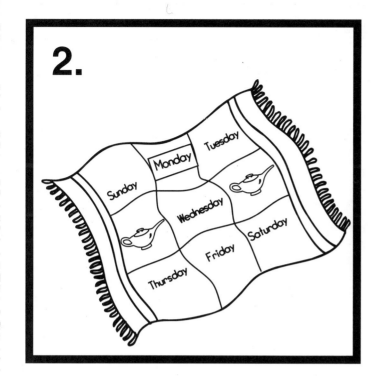

Aladdin

Matching Days of the Week

Directions:

Color magic carpet (page 96), mount on poster board, and store in pocket on center. Mount cards on poster board. Code backs with color dots to match carpet squares and cut apart. Store in plastic bag clipped to carpet with clothespins.

Students match cards to carpet squares.

Aladdin

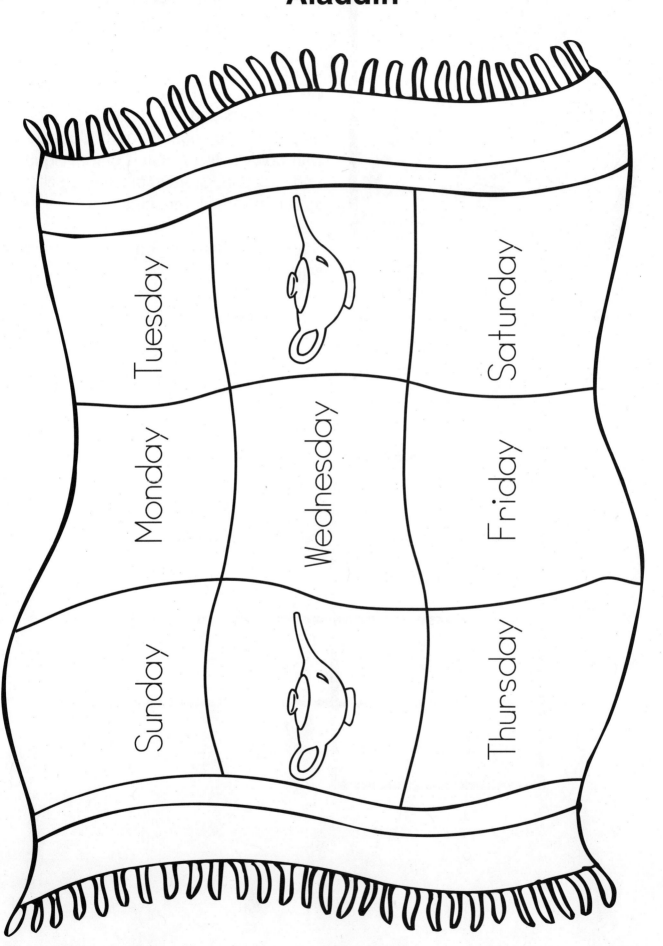

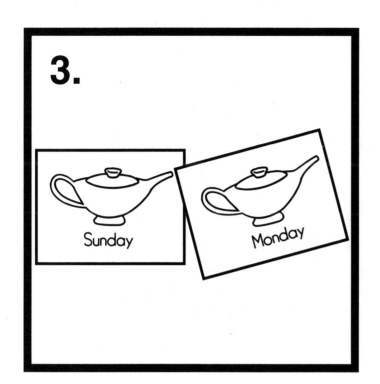

Aladdin
Ordering Days in Sequence

Directions:
Mount lamp shapes on poster board. Number backs for self-checking. Cut apart and store in pocket on center.

Students place the lamps in days-of-the-week order.

Aladdin

Tuesday

Wednesday

Thursday

Friday

Saturday

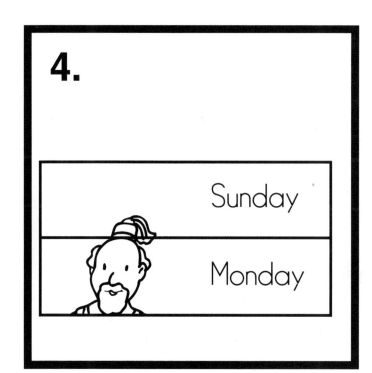

Aladdin
Ordering Days in Sequence

Directions:
Mount puzzle on poster board and laminate. Cut strips apart and store in pocket on center.

Students place strips in correct sequence.

Aladdin

Tuesday

Wednesday

Thursday

Friday

Saturday

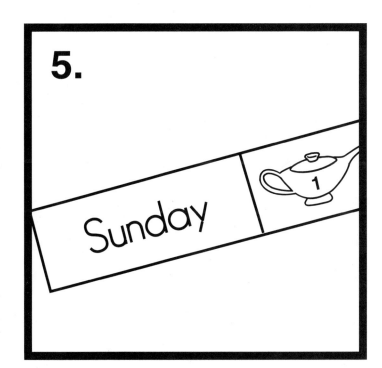

5.

Sunday

Aladdin
Selecting Days of the Week

Directions:
Duplicate numeral cards and chart. Cut apart. Store cards and charts in separate pockets on center. Provide paste for students to use.

Students match the numerals with the days of the week.

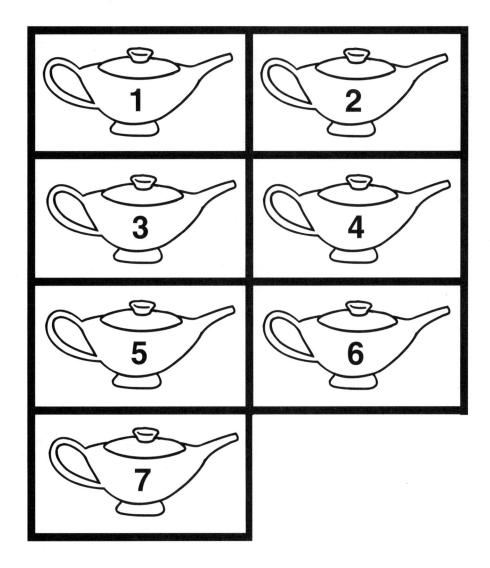

Aladdin

Sunday	
Monday	
Tuesday	
Wednesday	
Thursday	
Friday	
Saturday	

The Ugly Duckling
Comparing Sets

The Ugly Duckling

The Ugly Duckling

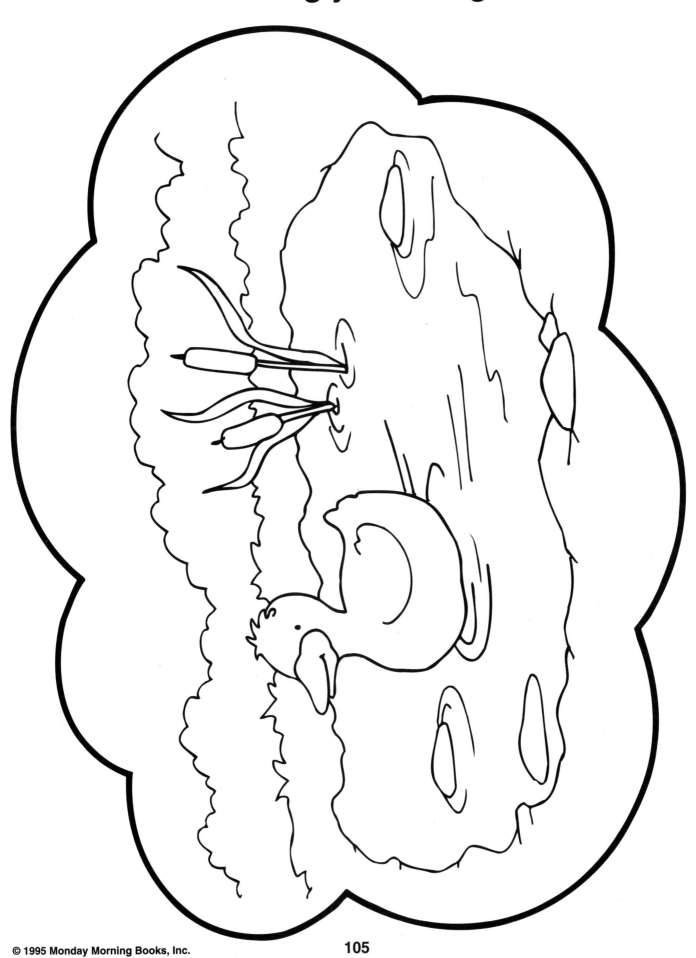

The Ugly Duckling

The Ugly Duckling
Drawing Lines to Match Sets

Directions:
Make a wipe-off pocket to hold activity sheets. Cut one piece of transparency acetate and one piece of construction paper slightly larger than activity sheet. Tape edges on three sides with masking tape. Slide activity sheet into pocket. Clip to center with clothespins. Provide wipe-off crayons and cleaning cloth. Update center by placing new activity sheets in wipe-off pockets.

Students draw lines to match sets.

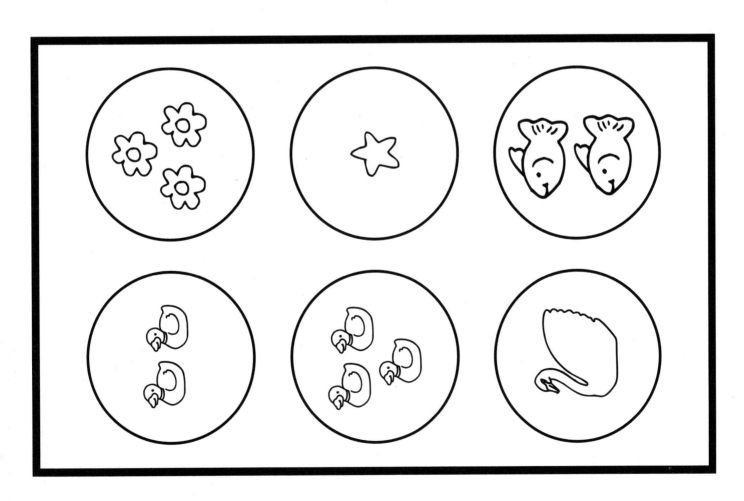

The Ugly Duckling

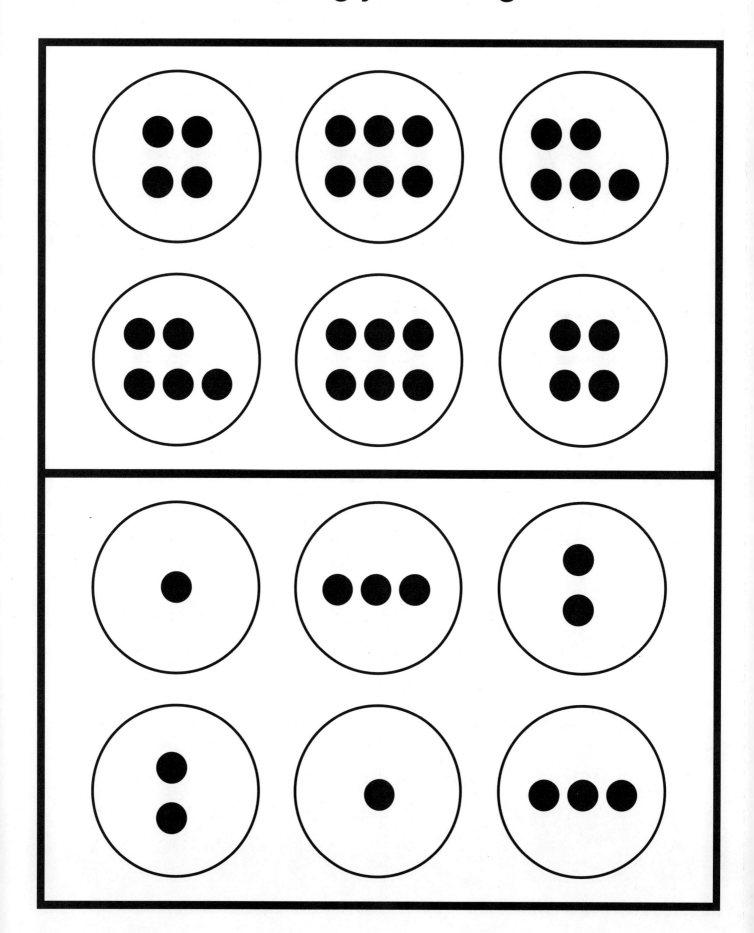

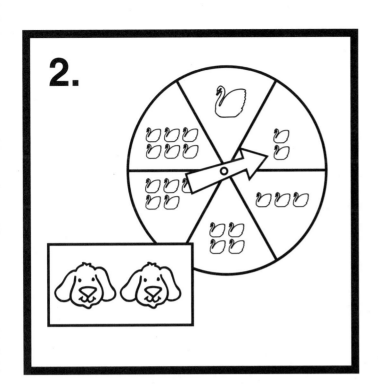

The Ugly Duckling
Matching Cards to Wheel

Directions:
Duplicate activity pictures. Cut apart and store in pocket on center. Mount wheel on center. Mount arrow on poster board and attach to wheel and center with 2-inch brad.

Students pick correct card to match wheel.

The Ugly Duckling

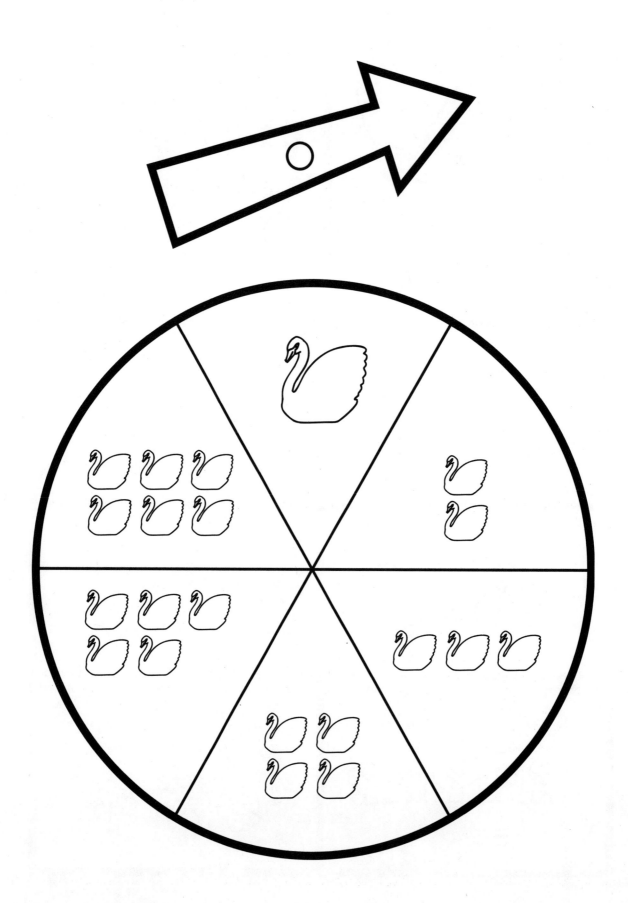

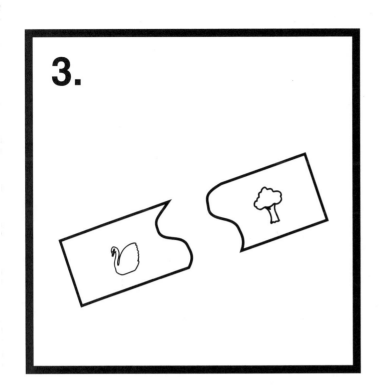

The Ugly Duckling
Matching Set Cards

Directions:
Mount puzzle pieces on poster board. Laminate, cut apart, and store in pocket on center.

Students fit pieces together to match sets.

The Ugly Duckling

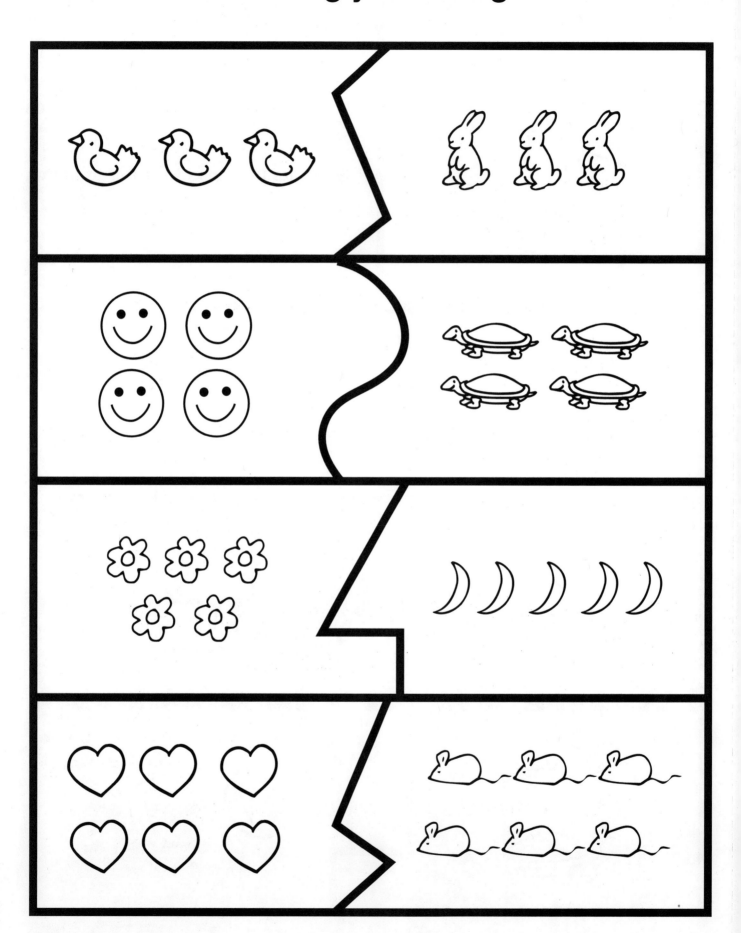

The Ugly Duckling
Pasting to Match Sets

Directions:
Duplicate set cards and cut apart. Store in pocket on center. Duplicate and cut apart activity cards. Store in separate pocket on center. Provide paste for students to use.

Students paste to match sets.

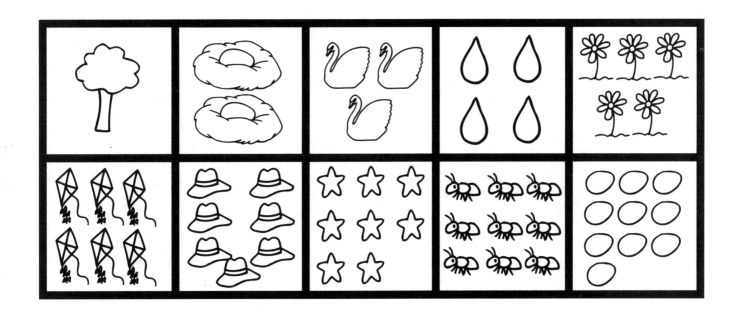

The Ugly Duckling

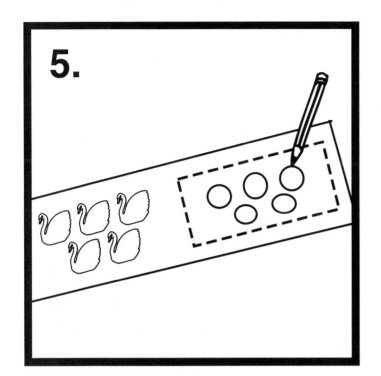

The Ugly Duckling
Drawing to Match Sets

Directions:
Duplicate activity pages. Cut apart and staple to form booklets. Store in pocket on center. Provide crayons for students to use..

Students draw to match sets.

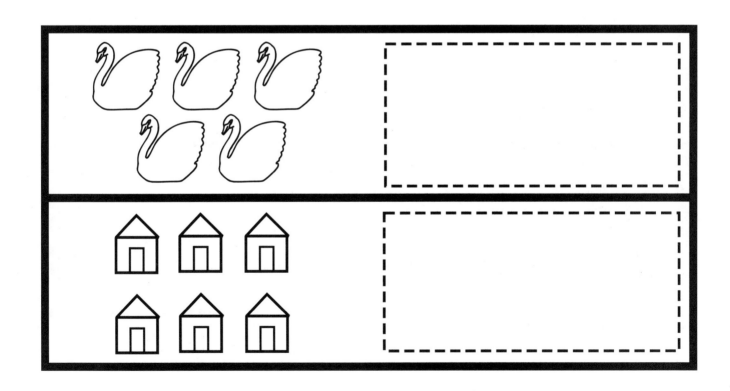

The Ugly Duckling

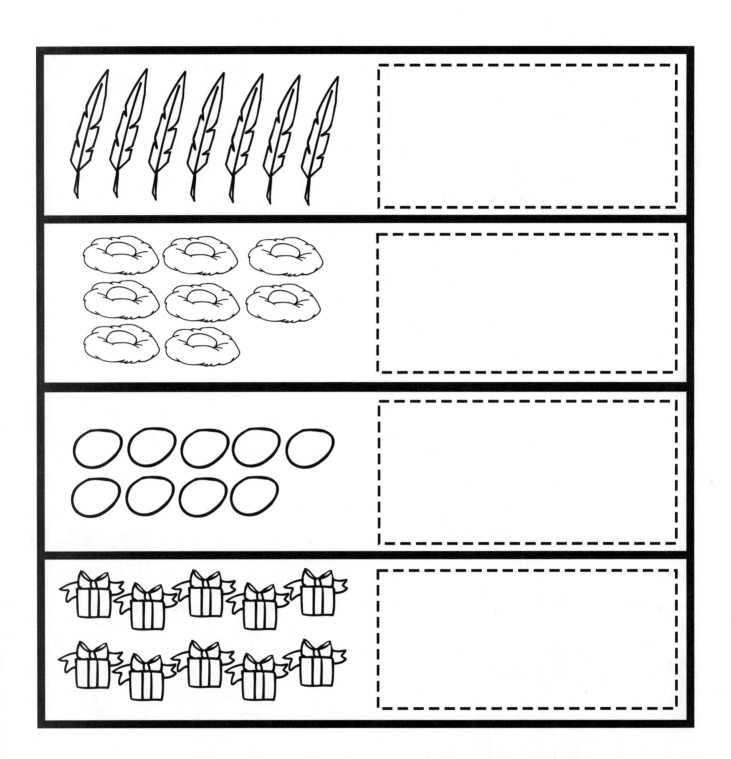

The Three Bears

Time

Materials:

2-inch brad   paste
construction paper   scissors
storage pockets   masking tape
transparency acetate   pinch clothespins
cleaning cloth   wipe-off crayons
poster board   crayons

The Three Bears

The Three Bears

119

The Three Bears

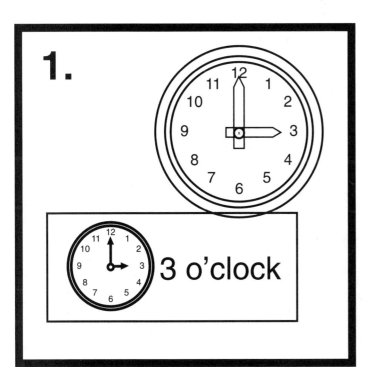

The Three Bears
Showing Time on a Clock

Directions:
Paste clock face on center. Mount hands on poster board and attach to clock with 2-inch brad. Duplicate time strips, cut apart, and store in pocket on center.

Students choose strips, then move hands on clock to show same time.

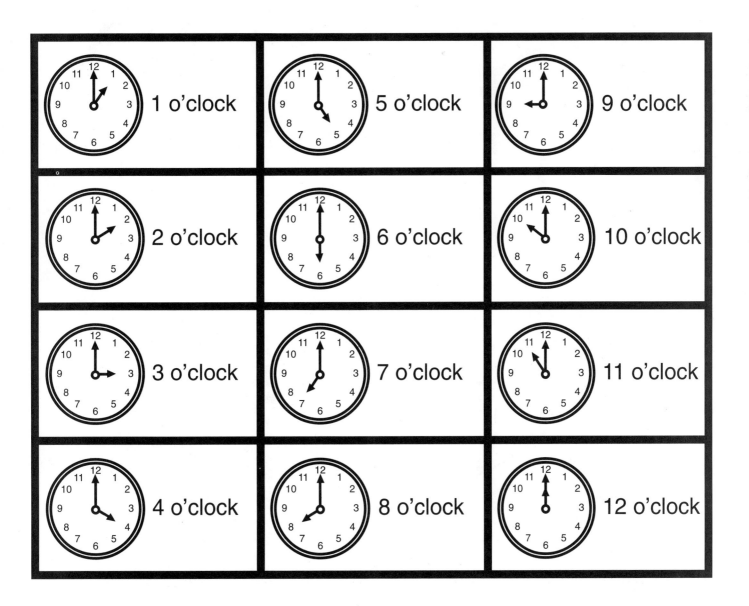

The Three Bears

The Three Bears

Selecting Hourly Activities

Directions:
Duplicate and cut out activity pictures and chart. Store in separate pockets on center. Provide paste for students to use.

Students paste activities to match time.

The Three Bears

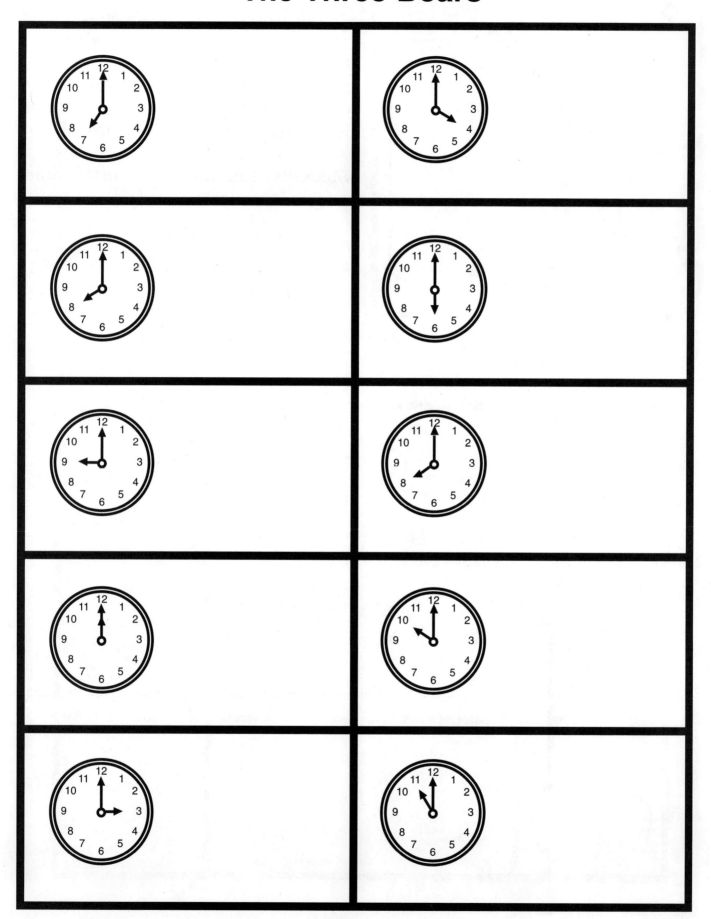

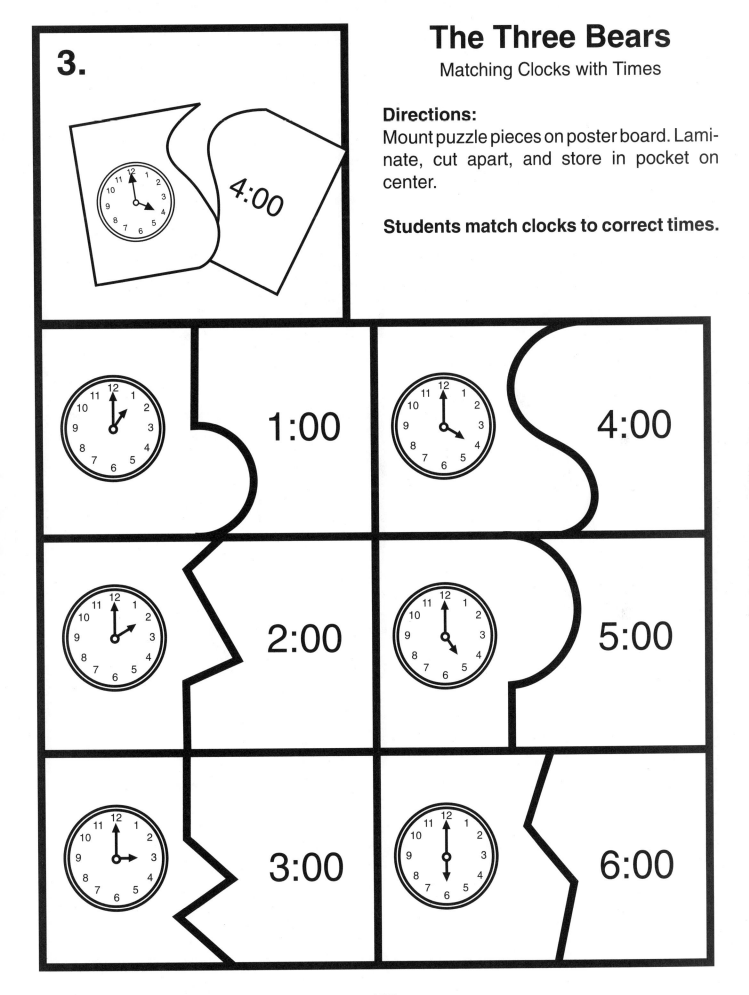

The Three Bears
Matching Clocks with Times

3.

Directions:
Mount puzzle pieces on poster board. Laminate, cut apart, and store in pocket on center.

Students match clocks to correct times.

4:00

1:00

4:00

2:00

5:00

3:00

6:00

The Three Bears

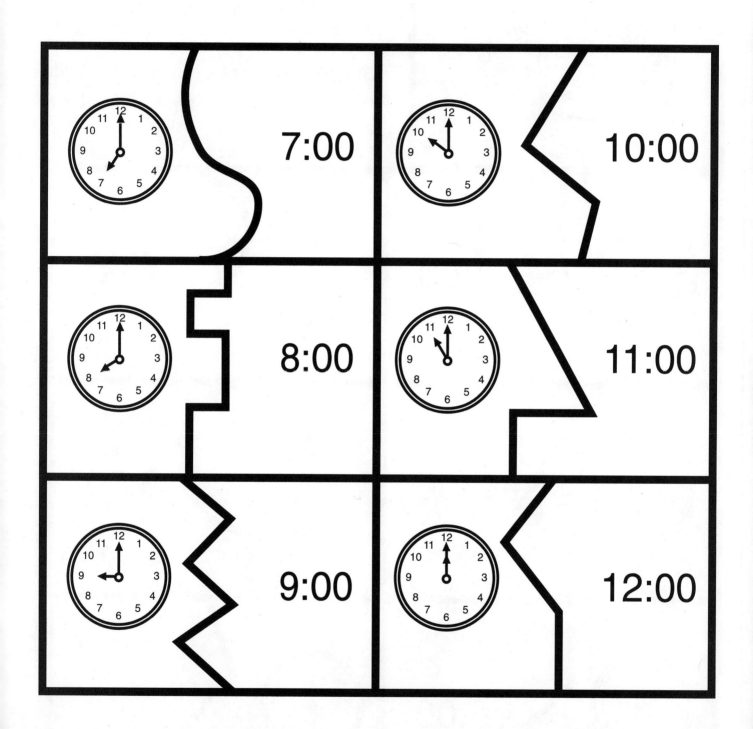

7:00

10:00

8:00

11:00

9:00

12:00

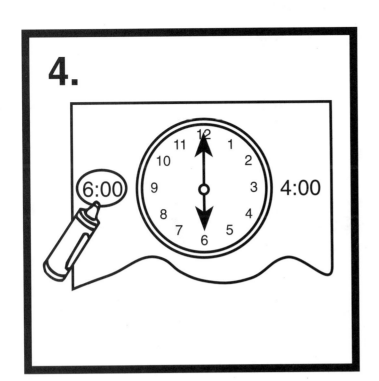

The Three Bears
Coloring the Correct Time

Directions:
Duplicate activity sheets. Cut apart and store in pocket on center. Provide crayons for students to use.

Students circle correct time.

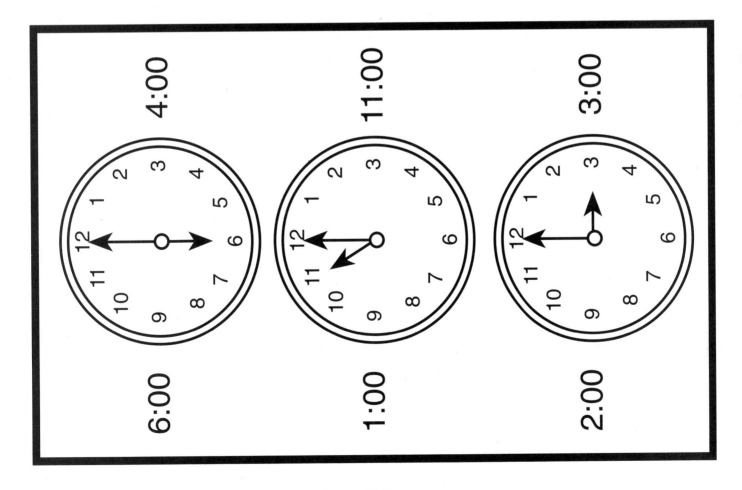

The Three Bears

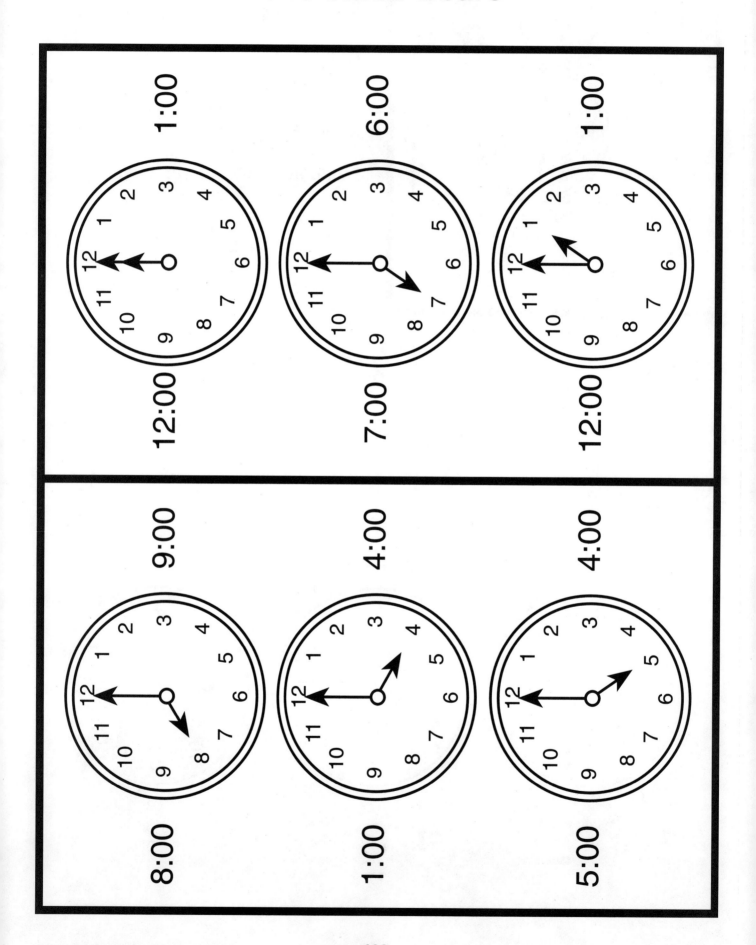

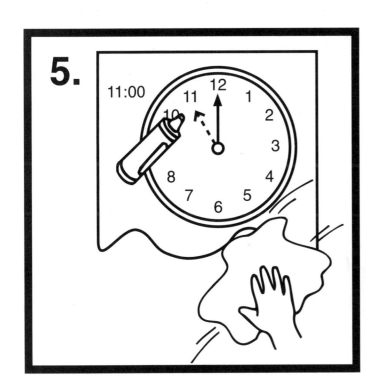

5.

The Three Bears
Drawing Missing Clock Hand

Directions:
Make wipe-off pocket to hold activity sheet. Cut one piece of transparency acetate and one piece of construction paper slightly larger than activity sheet. Tape edges on three sides with masking tape. Slide activity sheet into pocket. Clip to center with clothespins. Provide wipe-off crayon and cleaning cloth.

Students draw missing clock hands.

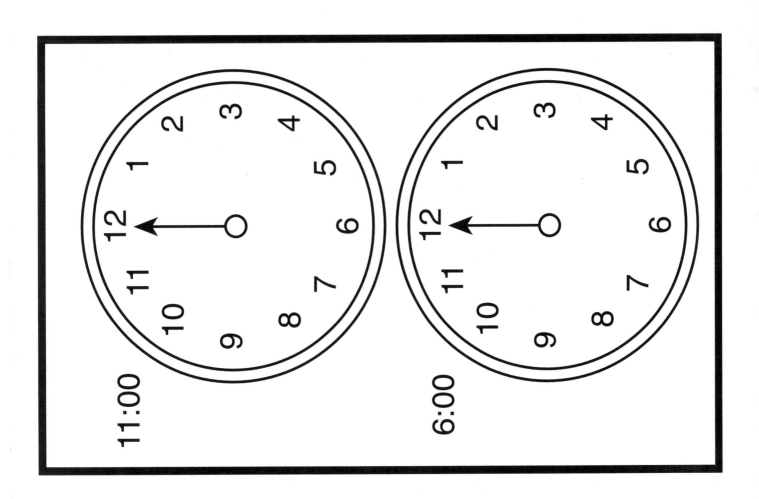

The Three Bears

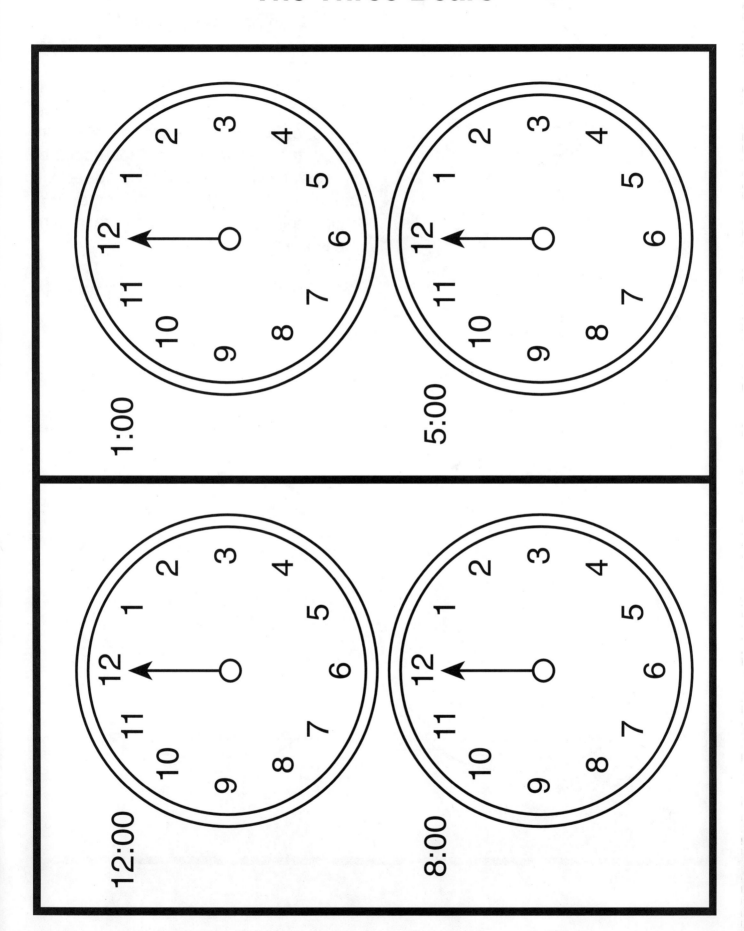

The City Mouse and the Country Mouse

Graphs

Materials:

storage pockets	crayons
jump rope	paste
small ball	scissors

The City Mouse and the Country Mouse

The City Mouse and the Country Mouse

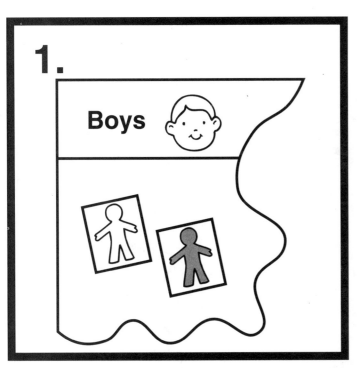

1.

Boys

The City Mouse and the Country Mouse

Completing Pictographs

Directions:

Duplicate symbol and graph sheets. Store in separate pockets on center. Provide scissors and paste.

Students cut apart and paste symbols to charts to make pictographs of their class.

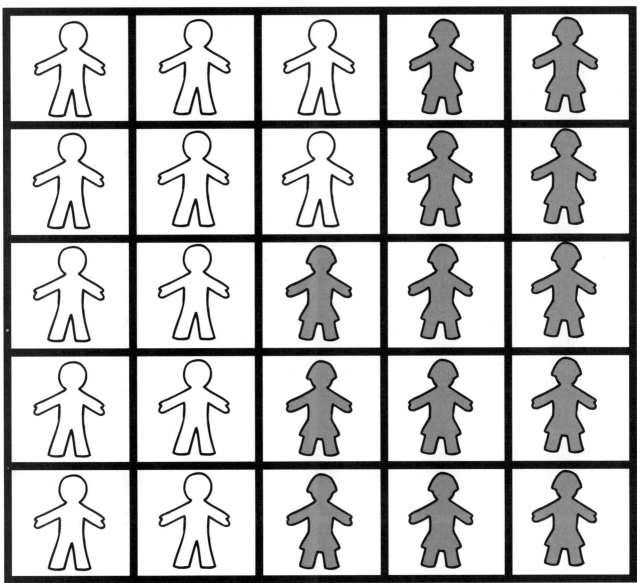

My Class

Boys	Girls

The City Mouse and the Country Mouse

Using Symbols

Directions:

Paste symbol key to center. Duplicate graph sheet and store in pocket on center.

Students draw in symbols to complete graph.

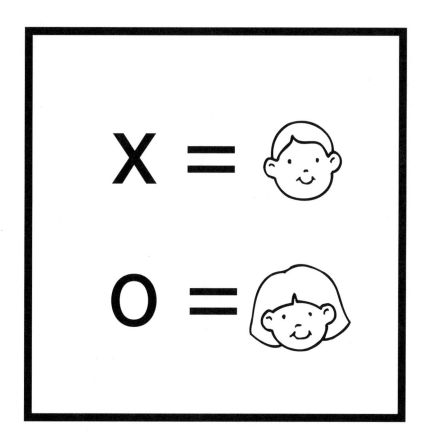

The City Mouse and the Country Mouse

I like cheese. ☺	I don't like cheese. ☹

The City Mouse and the Country Mouse

Graphing Data

Directions:
Mount scene on page 140 on center. Duplicate graph and store in pocket on center.

Students count items in scene and record on graph with crayons.

The City Mouse and the Country Mouse

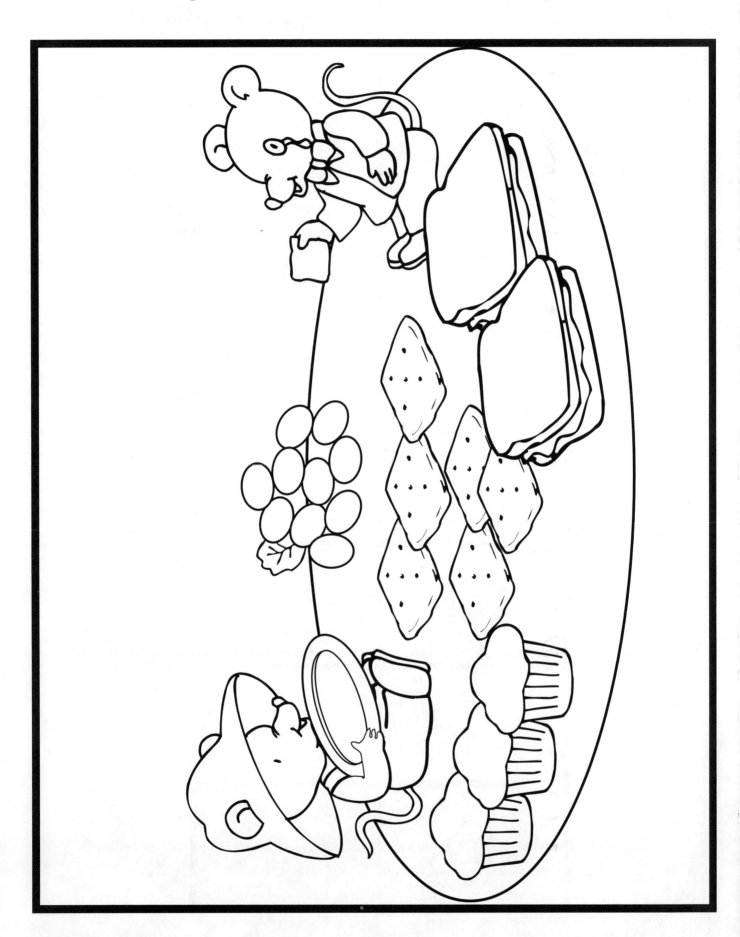

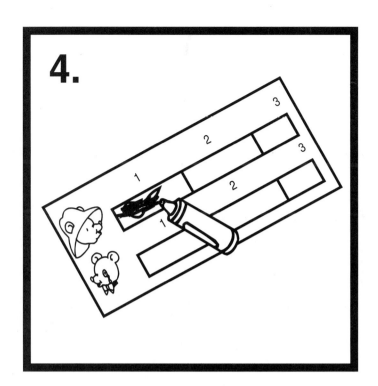

The City Mouse and the Country Mouse

Completing Bar Graph

Directions:

Mount illustration on center. Duplicate graphs and store in pocket on center. Cut apart activity cards

Students use crayons to fill in bars on graph indicating the number of stones the city mouse or the country mouse has jumped over.

141

The City Mouse and the Country Mouse

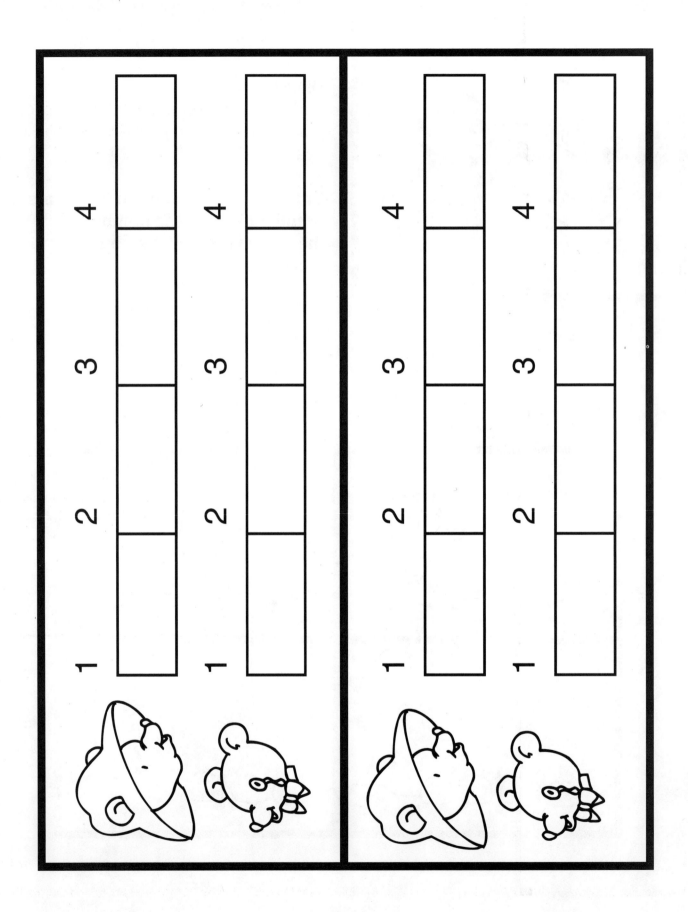

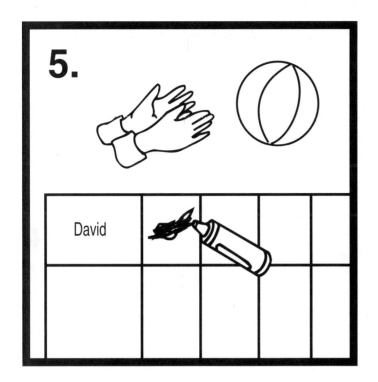

5.

David

The City Mouse and the Country Mouse
Completing Bar Graph

Directions:
Duplicate graphs and store in pocket on center. Provide ball, jump rope, and crayons for students to use to complete charts.

Students indicate the number of times they toss ball or jump rope.

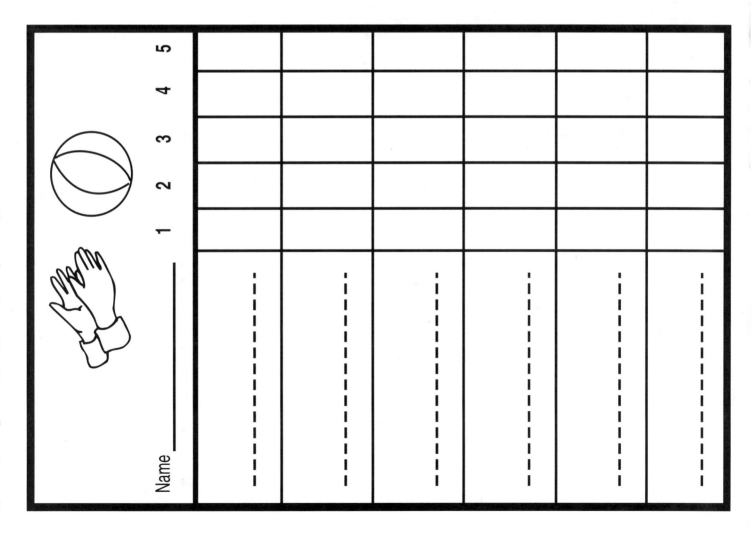

Name

The City Mouse and the Country Mouse

Name	1	2	3	4	5	6	7	8	9	10